SUFFER.

SUFFER.

JENNIFER K. CLARK, MD

MANUSCRIPTS
PRESS

COPYRIGHT © 2024 JENNIFER K. CLARK
All rights reserved.

SUFFER.

ISBN   979-8-88926-276-3 *Paperback*
           979-8-88926-232-9 *Hardcover*
           979-8-88926-230-5 *Ebook*

To my children

*may you know that you are safe,
may you know that you matter
as you discover who you are and
all the possibilities life may bring.
Welcome it all—the terrible and the sublime—
so that you may be fully known.
For it is there that wisdom will find you.*

Table of Contents

A NOTE BEFORE BEGINNING — 9
SUFFER. CHOOSE. CREATE. DIE. — 13

PART 1: **SUFFERING REIMAGINED** — 19
THE PROBLEM OF SUFFERING — 21
A NEW PARADIGM OF SUFFERING — 27
THE COMPASS OF SUFFERING — 39

PART 2: **SUFFERING AND SATISFACTION OF NEEDS** — 51
BASIC NEEDS AND THE SUFFERINGS OF SURVIVAL — 53
   FEAR. — 63
   SHAME. — 89
BECOMING NEEDS AND THE SUFFERINGS OF SELF — 121
   IGNORANCE. — 133
   JUDGMENT. — 157
BEING NEEDS AND THE SUFFERINGS OF SPIRIT — 179
   ISOLATION. — 185
   LONGING. — 211

PART 3: **SUFFERING AND SELF-ACTUALIZATION** — 237
TRANSCENDENCE — 239
PICKING UP THE COMPASS — 243
ACTUALIZATION SERIES — 247

ACKNOWLEDGMENTS — 249
END NOTES — 251

A Note before Beginning

…hope forged not from looking up or transcending difficulty or being saved, but rather from her own agency and imagination barreling through reality, refusing to surrender.

—LIDIA YUKNAVITCH, *THE MISFIT'S MANIFESTO*

Please allow me to first clarify, I do not seek to placate suffering. As the quote above states, "hope is not forged from looking up or transcending difficulty or being saved."[1] There is no choice in the happening of the most difficult, awful experiences of our lives. Trust me, the words "there is a reason" or "God has a plan" and all the other diverting euphemisms we use to address those who are suffering are not comforting; they hurt, and they are harmful. Under these well-intended words, the sufferer is not allowed to fully be seen or felt. In most cases the seer is too uncomfortable, so they reactively throw out these words like throwing a hand up to block out a blinding sun. Rather, this book is about hope, "hope forged…from agency and imagination," and how to make sense of this necessary human condition we call suffering.[2]

Stretching across the millennia of human existence, our great philosophical and religious traditions have aimed to solve the problem of suffering, yet here I am writing another tome dedicated to the topic. With humbled transparency, I will not be able to provide you with the answer to the burning question of the why of suffering, as alas that is out of my sphere of human capabilities. However, what I do know is that there is inherent power in suffering, and these pages seek to create a safe place for you to ease into its experiences and reimagine what it means in your own life.

Most of the stories shared here are from my best teachers—my patients. These stories have either been de-identified for privacy or represent an amalgamation of several people who shared common experiences. Recognizing that suffering contextualized by illness has primarily framed my thinking, I have strived to be conscientious of the implicit historical patriarchy in healthcare and its consequential influence on medical education and practice. Additionally, I also want to be sensitive to the fact our society frequently monetizes suffering. Where healthcare is a monolith to disease in a society that values monetary worth, purposefully attending to the subject of suffering is to accept the risks of walking through a minefield full of latent, disastrous misunderstandings.

Science, religion, and philosophy have also undoubtedly influenced my draw to and understanding of life's sorrows. My Celtic-Catholic childhood, filled with icons and rituals of suffering, have undoubtedly established deep-rooted, unconscious ways of seeing the world. Further, my professional years have been peppered with various forays into Human-Centered Design, Ayurveda, Systems Thinking,

Secular Buddhism, Stoicism, Humanistic Psychology, and the list goes on. I am a human and therefore flawed, and what follows are my reflections and observations on a life lived as a healer.

All this to say, I am willing, able, and well-intentioned to walk with you in suffering, and I beg of you some grace. The reading will not be easy. Take it slowly. Please seek help when and where you need it.

Suffer. Choose. Create. Die.

Oh joy, if it isn't Suffering's handmaiden!
—DR. P, A PSYCHIATRIST FRIEND, SAID TO ME UPON ARRIVING AT OUR SHARED PATIENT'S ROOM

At 7:02 a.m. on a cold November Monday, my companionship with Suffering took an unexpected turn. As typical, I was engrossed in a book while drinking my morning coffee. My mom, who had been staying with us following the separation between her and my dad, came running into the kitchen, wild-eyed with fear.

"What is this?" she screamed, shoving her phone into my face.

Aggravated with my mom's lifelong tendency toward the dramatic, I took the phone. Little did I know that in that moment, my life would be rendered to near obliteration. My dad's words glowed on the page, a confused message of deep heartache and goodbye.

Then it dawned on me. My dad was dead. He had taken his own life.

It seemed Suffering was knocking on the door that morning as a visitor rather than as my companion, and I was now being called to muster the courage to trust the message Suffering had to offer.

As a hospice and palliative medicine physician, I have accompanied Suffering on many visits to those living through distressful change and loss. Grief brings an invisible, weighted fog that shrouds those it touches. When flavored with trauma, the fog can be deeply painful and suffocating. Intellectually and compassionately, I have sat with others with the weight of traumatic grief, but when the shroud wrapped itself around my own shoulders, I came to realize that though I had been *in* those visits to console and support, I was not *of* them. A layer of emotional inexperience had been blunting my ability to fully appreciate the depth, breadth, and range of emotions involved in the death of a loved one, especially one so traumatic. The direct experience is crushing. Brené Brown, researcher and storyteller, fully captures this in her definition of anguish:

> "Anguish not only takes away our ability to breathe, feel, and think—it comes for our bones. Anguish often causes us to physically crumple in on ourselves, literally bringing us to our knees or forcing us all the way to the ground. The element of powerlessness

is what makes anguish traumatic: We are unable to change, reverse, or negotiate what has happened."[1]

Slowly, in the days and weeks following my dad's suicide, anguish carved its way through me and finally began to ease its hold on my body and mind as the voices of friends and family began to ring with the other familiar messages of Suffering that have so often passed my own lips—messages of love, honesty, hope, faith, and even joy. Eventually, following the necessary yet painfully prolonged stay, Suffering's visit ended. Suffering rejoined me as a professional companion. With a new depth of intimacy, our shared adventures are now ineffably rich and dynamic. It seems the visit instilled a fortitude and capacity for me to travel roads previously inaccessible. Like a musician who surrenders to bring forth the alchemical power of Music, I am now a healer who surrenders to bring forth the same said power of Suffering. Serving as a beacon of light, Suffering's compassion shined the path forward and, eventually, the shattered pieces of my life began to reform into something wholly new.

As the wake of grief subsides and grieving begins, mortality salience, the awareness of our own impermanence, opens us to see life from a different perspective. A powerful developmental tool, mortality salience creates a map of one's life between the lands of birth and death that gives us an appreciation of where we have been, where we are, and where we are going. From this map we navigate making amends with the past and living intentionally in the present while fostering the wherewithal to embrace the future that inevitably includes death. Now, through my own experience of anguish, I understand that suffering is the compass that allows for the wise navigation of life's choices and vacillations, the markings on our life's map.

Due to our deep societal fears and intolerance of discomfort, the messages of suffering are frequently met with a combination of fear, profound ignorance, or immense vitriol and disgust. Nearly everyone believes suffering should be avoided at all costs and, in fact, many people limit living to mitigate their chances of meeting with suffering. However, on the occasion when a patient, colleague, student, or friend has had the courage to hear suffering's message and brave the step toward rather than away, I have seen the vast beauty and transcendent power of suffering and its ability to positively transform a human life. This phenomenon has transfixed my scientific mind for over two decades, but through my own direct experience, I was afforded the language to better study and recognize suffering's purpose.

Working with suffering in the context of exploring the highest potential of human development provides an odd juxtaposition, but it now serves as the basis for my practice as a physician and my existence as a human. Through this new way of living and practicing, I have come to see a universal cycle of suffering, choosing, creating, and dying that empowers our drive toward self-actualization.

Picking up the compass of suffering is a courageous act, as it requires the vulnerability to consciously choose to move toward those things we most wish to avoid. Interestingly, it seems we all try to avoid the same things. Suffering's various flavors of fear, shame, ignorance, judgment, isolation, and longing define what most of us routinely steer clear of. After spending time with those who have chosen to pick up the compass, I began to see a secondary pattern. Each of suffering's universal flavors reflects a human need that has gone materially unmet. The consistent satisfaction of the essential needs of safety, connection, esteem, exploration, intimacy, and purpose is necessary for optimal human development, and when compromised, we suffer.

In seeing the relationship between suffering and the satisfaction of needs, a framework arose. Built on direct experience supported by science, philosophy, religion, and a millennium of human life, the framework deploys the sufferings of survival, self, and spirit as the cardinal directions of the compass, guiding conscious human development. The framework is the basis of this book.

Perhaps you have picked up this book because you are amid one of life's great transitions, or maybe you're living through the grief and grieving of a recent loss. You might be a caregiver or loved one of someone who is suffering and feel helpless in supporting them, or you just might be someone who is really curious about what it means to live a fully actualized life. For all those reasons and more, these pages are intended to be a compassionate yet candid container for you to explore the most tender places of your existence.

Like the individuals, audiences, and organizations with whom this work has already been shared, may your reading foster the courage to embrace your mortality, suffer well, choose wisely, and bravely harness the power of the human condition to create a fully human life.

PART 1:

SUFFERING REIMAGINED

The Problem of Suffering

SUFFERING SUFFERS A PROBLEM OF LANGUAGE
I realize that definitions spark controversy and disagreement, but I'm okay with that. I'd rather we debate the meaning of words that are important to us than not discuss them at all. We need common language to help us create awareness and understanding, which is essential to Wholehearted living.
—BRENÉ BROWN, *THE GIFTS OF IMPERFECTIONS*

At the edge of mortality, life is really alive. The minutiae are wiped away and truth comes to bear. Inherently, I think that is what initially drew me into hospice and palliative medicine, but the paradoxical unifying experience of loss drew me to embrace the power of suffering. Like the Japanese art of wabi-sabi, which loosely translates to the attentive melancholy of finding the beauty in impermanence, the power of suffering unifies the dissolution of loss with the creation of something entirely new.[1]

What I have come to understand, though, is that suffering suffers a problem of language. It's too obscure and, like death, it feels taboo.

As a young physician, I was desperate to understand the phenomenon of suffering, and early in my practice, I was fortunate enough to be taught by Dr. Eric Cassell, celebrated physician and author of *The Nature of Suffering and the Goals of Medicine*. First published as an article in the esteemed *New England Journal of Medicine*, Cassell's view of suffering became an essential teaching of the nascent medical subspecialty of hospice and palliative medicine. Later, when his work was expanded to book form, *The Nature of Suffering and the Goals of Medicine* went on to inform many fields beyond those primarily focused on medical ethics and clinical practice.

His enigmatic gaze, intellectual brilliance, and dry wit made him the best of teachers. He taught and mentored me in the practice of addressing a patient as a person with goals and purpose, framing the focus of my therapeutic work as seeking out and mitigating those things that interfered with growth and flourishing. To this end, Cassell was the first to introduce me to the "distinction…between suffering and physical distress" and the relief of suffering as one of the "primary ends of medicine."[2]

When hearing the word *suffer*, many people visibly flinch. It has an onomatopoeic quality, as it calls to the pain and anguish of the typically imagined receiving of a terminal cancer diagnosis, enduring of a traumatic injury, or bearing the destruction of a natural disaster. Webster supports this in its definition of suffer as a verb:

To Suffer

to be subject to disability or handicap

to sustain loss or damage

At this point *suffer* as a word begins to be flummoxed by a hidden element of assumed passivity embedded in its working definition, as Webster continues:

to submit to or be forced to endure, particularly things like death, pain, or distress

to undergo, experience

to put up, with especially as inevitable or unavoidable

to allow, especially by reason of indifference

to feel keenly: labor under

Consequently, this language creates two basic yet interrelated expressions of what it means to suffer. As given in Webster's example sentences:

- One refers to a causal event, a factual statement:
    - "He *suffered* a heart attack and died instantly."
- The other opens up the door to an individual's context of the causal event:
    - "He died instantly and did not *suffer*."

By themselves, external events like injury, illness, trauma, or loss are neutral. This also applies to internal streams of information such as sensations like pain, emotions, thoughts, images, and feelings. Together, external events and internal streams of information create experiences, some of which we causally suffer. However, when said experiences are contextualized within our lives, the occasion for the second aspect of suffering arises. Eloquently captured in a well-known Buddhist parable of the two arrows:

> "If a person is struck by an arrow, is it painful?
>
> If the person is struck by a second arrow, is it even more painful?
>
> In life, we can't always control the first arrow. However, the second arrow is our reaction to the first.
>
> This second arrow is optional."[3]

The second arrow, the suffering of suffering, is the subject of this book.

THE SUFFERING OF SUFFERING

The events of suffering will always exist, but the suffering of suffering, we can be released from its power.
—JACK KORNFIELD, *THE WISE HEART*

The suffering of suffering continues down the tricky path of language, fraught with confusion between the cause and the object of suffering. To better rectify the distinction between the cause and the object of suffering, Cassell layered his definition of suffering on the prerequisite of personhood. He believed suffering was a distressful state related to events that pose a threat to the "intactness of a person."[4] Cassell insisted that personhood is primarily shaped by the human abilities to perceive the full expanse of time, imagine a future, articulate meaning to events, and act autonomously. Controversially, he concluded that individuals without these abilities, such as infants, those living with dementia, traumatic brain injuries, developmental disabilities, and the like, cannot suffer. As eloquently stated by Cassell's critics, his definition of suffering is "exclusive to linguistically competent beings with high degrees of agency."[5]

My primary training involved both internal medicine and pediatrics. Termed med-peds for short, this training exposed me to care across the entire age continuum. Extended to my subspecialty certification and practice in hospice and palliative medicine, I have cared for seriously ill and dying people over an age spectrum ranging from thirteen weeks utero to one hundred eight years old. Having borne witness to extremes of the human condition across all ages, my belief is that suffering is suffering is suffering, regardless of the ability to articulate or mitigate it. Needless to say, Cassell and I agreed to disagree on this point.

Others have worked to further rectify this cause and object conundrum of suffering. Aligned with the formal definition of suffering, unmuddied by personhood, expressive language capacity, and dependency, Dr. Tyler VanderWeele, director of Harvard's Human Flourishing Program, offers: "The cause of the suffering is the event that has brought about the suffering, the object of suffering being that over which there is physical, psychological, or existential distress…"[6]

We see this tension play out each day in the intensive care units of our hospitals. Intubated, sedated, and unable to communicate, patients facing a life-threatening event are surrounded by family asking the heart-aching question, "Are they suffering?"

The confusion of causation does point to the heart of the problem of suffering…*how, what, or who determines when a difficult experience shifts from unpleasant discomfort to one of suffering?* Are there universal qualities or contexts that the majority of us subjectively consider suffering, hence making them slide toward a point of objectivity? Perhaps.

A New Paradigm of Suffering

> *...the most obvious, ubiquitous, important realities are often the ones that are hardest to see and talk about.*
> —DAVID FOSTER WALLACE, "THIS IS WATER"

NAMING THE WATER

In 2005 at Kenyon College, author and philosopher David Foster Wallace gave the commencement address entitled "This Is Water." In it, he famously describes a cartoon scene where an older, wiser fish swims up on two younger fish and offers a question regarding the state of the water that morning. Horribly confused, the two younger fish continue swimming until one of them quizzically asks the other, "What the hell is water?"[1]

This simple yet powerful image poignantly displays the often-ineffable roots of human suffering. "Naming the water" is one of the most useful metaphors to use when jumping into the work of deep pain, sorrow, and dissatisfaction, and I have come to believe that the naming of one's suffering is the essential first step in the transformation of its power. Naming mollifies the confusing issue of language in suffering. As a colleague once summarized, "Now that I can name it, I can manage it. If I don't acknowledge it, I can't wrestle with it."[2]

In the wake of my father's death, I revisited much of the ethical, philosophical, and religious literature on suicide to better understand and extend compassion toward my dad's suffering and its consequential end. During this search, I stumbled across Wallace's work, as he also died by his own hand just a few short years following the address at Kenyon. Wallace's philosophy centers on two questions:

> "How do we keep from going through adult life unconsciously, comfortably entrenched in habit?
>
> How do we remove ourselves from the foreground of our thoughts and achieve compassion?"[3]

For me, these two questions shaped a clearer understanding of suffering. As called out by these questions, suffering is a multilayered experience with universal qualities that then develop into more predictable patterns with individuated manifestations. The reimagining of suffering begins with the consideration of its universal patterns or more coquettishly, the naming of its water.

THE UNIVERSAL NATURE OF SUFFERING
Without suffering and death, a human life cannot be complete.
— VIKTOR FRANKL, *MAN'S SEARCH FOR MEANING*

We are *Homo sapiens sapiens,* the man who knows he knows. The known world is chaotic and unpredictable, and the human capability "to know" comes with profound upsides and equally disturbing downsides. The upside, unlike any other species that we are aware of, is that humans are afforded the abilities to imagine, to make meaning, and to create all on a basis of beliefs and values. The equally painful downside, unlike any other species that we are aware of, is that humans are afforded the abilities to imagine, to make meaning, and to create all on a basis of beliefs and values. The price "to know" is suffering.

The universality of suffering begins with the anatomy and physiology of the human nervous system. We are equipped with a three-part brain. The first part of the brain is the brainstem, our most rudimentary or reptilian brain. It is responsible for our survival and safety. It kicks in when you're sleeping at night and allows you to breathe or pulls your hand away from a hot stove.

The second part is our mammalian brain, which consists of the more complex regulatory systems involving hormones and neurotransmitters. It is also the home of our memories and emotions. Finally, the third and newest part represents the unique human brain where cognition, planning, and other executive functions are at play. Simply, we are creatures primarily wired for security and survival sprinkled with an added bonus of insight.

Received through our body's sensory system, experiences are primarily filtered through the unconscious bottom and middle parts of the brain, and only on rare occasion do experiences percolate up to be made conscious in our human brain. This means that the majority of life experiences are generated in the lower parts of our brain, rendering us, as Wallace describes, "unconsciously entrenched in habit."

Unconsciously, we primarily navigate the world with the two antennae of salience and valence. Salience is the ability for something to attract our attention, and valence reflects our instinctual assessment of threat. These antennae probe the world in search of disaster, unconsciously driving our every move. Together, these functions formulate the general feeling tone of our experience—this is good, this is bad, this is meh.

For example, let's take the benign but intense experience of a paper cut. Imagine the moment the sensation of pain and sight of blood saliently draw your attention to the site of injury. In rapid sequence, the valent perception of threat immediately follows, manifesting with the likely shouting of an expletive and the all-too-common reactive finger-to-mouth tending of the wound. Overall, the feeling generated is usually not so good.

On scale, the salience involved in an experience of suffering is extremely intense, capturing our full attention, and with it, the valence renders an equally extreme sense of threat.

At the bedsides of those I serve, I hear the echoes of this in those recalled moments where their lives turned on a dime. From the salience of the three words "you have cancer" to the valence of mortal threat in understanding their lives will be forever changed, I've held the space for the torrent of emotions and instinctual reactions to unfold.

Consistently, the salience and valence of these moments seemingly shape a shared language of negative feeling tone that patients use to name their suffering. Across the years of my practice, patients have universally described the feeling tone of suffering as unwanted, uncontrollable, and unbearable:

> **Unwanted:** As alluded to with the notion of valence, the causal experiences leading to suffering have a threatening quality and are often perceived to be associated with an attack or injury caused by force from "beyond" ourselves. Disruptive of relationships to self, others, or the world at large, these experiences are wholly unwelcome.

> **Uncontrollable.** The causal aspects of our suffering are often felt to be outside of our control, leaving a residue of powerlessness. Desperate for relief, our system releases an avalanche of instinctual and impulsive reactions, many of which are protectively barred from conscious recognition. If unrelieved, the suffering is painfully ineffable, as it can claim our independent functioning, stripping our capacity for agency and autonomy.

Unbearable: Dealing with even a modicum of discomfort is a significant issue in modern life, as there appears to be a false narrative that all things unpleasant are wrong. Putting this issue of tolerance aside, in terms of suffering, the degree of unpleasantness goes far beyond the necessary discomforts of learning, striving, minor injury, or illness, and the distress of suffering involves an intense pervasiveness of undefined duration, collapsing the experiencer under its weight.

As humans, like our reptilian and mammalian cousins, we all experience the salience and valence of suffering, but unlike those cousins, we are also equipped with the capacity to create meaning. And herein lies the individuated experiences of suffering as an all-encompassing threat that triggers the more elaborate human cognitive function of storytelling. An evolutionarily adaptive function, storytelling, even in its most primitive form, attempts to help us make sense of the world. In this case, attending to the unwanted, uncontrollable, and unbearable threats is further shaped by a narrative of why we must endure such difficulty. While adaptively intended, these narratives and their resulting qualities of mind may not always provide relief and may actually compound the agony of the experience, launching the suffering of suffering into an endless, self-perpetuating cycle.

This meaning-making harkens to Wallace's second inquiry that refers to the how of "[removing] ourselves from the foreground of our thoughts." With meaning, the universal suffering of suffering becomes much more personal, intimate.

Because of this too personal and intimate nature, we seem to hold suffering at an intellectual distance, avoiding its direct experience and losing out on the opportunity to engage with its transformative capacities.

While naming the problem of suffering, its neurobiological underpinnings, and universal qualities may help talk about "the most obvious, ubiquitous, important realities" of our lives as humans, what is to be done about it?[4]

SUFFERING IS A CALL TO ATTEND TO OUR MOST FUNDAMENTAL NEEDS

Self-actualizing people, those who have come to a high level of maturation, health, and self-fulfillment, have so much to teach us that sometimes they seem almost like a different breed of human being.
— ABRAHAM MASLOW, *TOWARD A PSYCHOLOGY OF BEING*

While naming provides therapeutic clarity on the nature of one's suffering, it still remains an unwanted, unbearable, and uncontrollable force in one's life that calls to be directed. I spent my young adulthood grappling to understand the why, what, and how of suffering but not until I met Lily did the pieces of the suffering puzzle begin to fall into place.

As a young palliative care attending, I was asked to participate in Lily's care. She was a vivacious twenty-five-year-old who carried a diagnosis of aggressive multiple sclerosis. Amid her numerous journeys in and out of the hospital, we came to know each other over the course of a couple of years. Despite a heavy burden of disease, Lily exuded a confident wisdom that belied her chronological age. Her wisdom and dry sense of humor endeared her to all of us who cared for her. Some days, the physical pain left her writhing. On others, the disconnection from the routines and rituals of young adult life saddled her with heartache or the longing for a future that would never come to pass.

Her soul was stripped bare. However, not infrequently, she would possess an unending well of strength to host a stream of visitors that clogged the hospital hallways with what felt like the riotousness of a college dorm, or she would joyfully sit in intimate one-on-one conversations whispering about her beliefs, values, and meanings, leaving her companions deeply moved. She never held back. She suffered well, and she was satisfied, allowing the fullness of experience to flow through her. For me, Lily exemplified what it means to live a self-actualized life.

Med-peds residency combines in-depth medical training with the added lens of human development. Many of my similarly schooled colleagues enter this type of training to hone their skills in treating diseases that stretch across the age continuum. This training exposed me to several developmental frameworks and sparked a lifelong interest in human flourishing.

The rapidly growing science of flourishing, well-being, and positive psychology has been exciting to watch unfold. Through these efforts, we are finally addressing the physically reductionist model of health that has underpinned modern medicine since its inception. No doubt the healers of the body-mind split—from William James to the existential-humanistic psychologists like Viktor Frankl, Carl Rogers, and the modern-day positive psychologist, Martin Seligman—would be thrilled to see the vast legacy of their work continuing to expand and influence the far reaches of human life.

For me, though, Abraham Maslow and his hierarchy of needs continually resonate deeply within my own developmental experiences as well as within the direct experiences of caring for seriously ill and dying people. Maslow's language is easily relatable and packed with nuggets of brilliance. Little explanation is required to understand the needs for physical safety, connection and belonging, and strong self-esteem. Even with the more nuanced needs of exploration, intimacy, and purpose, Maslow masterfully describes what motivates us to mature.

Maslow believed that each need, when left unsatisfied, creates a hypervigilant "drive and behavior, with the one unqualified aim of relief."[5] Because of the survival and security mechanisms of the lower brain functions, we are motivated by this hypervigilant need for relief. From this viewpoint, we can think of suffering as the ultimate expression of an unmet need, and perhaps, this gives us the required objective and universal language to collectively understand and engage with the suffering of suffering.

Stan van Hooft, an internationally recognized professor of philosophy and bioethics, offers the closest portrayal of suffering in this manner. In his 1998 response to Cassell's work and his influence on the Hastings Center, the oldest nonprofit organization dedicated to nonpartisan bioethics, van Hooft uses the four-part Aristotelian framework of the soul to shape his view of suffering. The article beautifully addresses the problematic causal confusion of suffering, but van Hooft continues an error of confabulating suffering within the context of the goals of medicine, and the use of the framework gets somewhat muddled. However, van Hooft opened the door to the opportunity to think of suffering beyond the rudimentary borders of pain and anguish, in that he offers:

> "We must also consider the internal, existential goal of the integration of our lives which I map onto Aristotle's model as the tendency to achieve the wholeness of the four aspects of our being... One feels the vigor of health in so far as one enjoys happy relationships with others, feels at home in the world, is engaged in tasks that hold reasonable promise of success and which have a meaning in one's larger conception of life. Anything that frustrates the tendency to create this wholeness in one's life will constitute suffering."[6]

To this end, through Maslow's plain yet elegant language and its profound display in Lily, I began to see a parallel between the hierarchy of needs and the experiences of suffering. Lily, by all traditional terms, was "suffering." She was a twenty-five-year-old who was dying and in pain. Yet her suffering was different from the other young adults I'd cared for, as many of them had seemingly lost varying degrees of their maturity and a few even totally collapsed into childlike helplessness under the weight of disease. Even on her worst days and, arguably, mostly on her worst days, Lily flourished. "Pain is pain, death is death, neither of which I am interested in allowing to define me," she said. "My heart longs, exquisitely so. I want it all—the good, bad, and ugly."

Her use of the statement "my heart longs, exquisitely so" provoked the inquiry that led to the writing of this book.

Flourishing. Satisfaction. Frustration. Suffering.

The language all points to an objective matter of needs and, therefore, a potential framework for harnessing the power of suffering to meaningfully create our lives. Shifting the paradigm from its historical place as an avoid-at-all cost evil to one of an appreciated superpower, suffering, once named, is simply a call to attend to our most fundamental needs.

The Compass
of Suffering

———

REVISITING MASLOW

One can choose to go back toward safety or forward toward growth. Growth must be chosen again and again; fear must be overcome again and again.
—ABRAHAM MASLOW, TOWARD A PSYCHOLOGY OF BEING

Maslow's hierarchy of needs, first published in 1943, outlines a theory of human motivation that has stood the test of time, and despite its lack of preliminary research, has remained foundational to our understanding of human life. Scott Barry Kaufman, a modern humanistic psychologist, rediscovered Maslow's unpublished writing and provided an update to the hierarchy in his book *Transcend*. In it, Kaufman not only debunks the hierarchy-as-a-pyramid myth and offers a more workable sailboat analogy, but he also introduces a modernized hierarchy of needs that incorporates the previously lacking body of science, which has exponentially grown since Maslow's death in 1970.[1]

Maslow's theory, further shaped by Kaufman, makes a clear distinction between "deficiency needs" and "growth needs" as well as their influence on development.[2] Deficiency needs—safety, connection, and esteem—motivate us to survive. Growth needs—exploration, intimacy, and purpose—motivate us to thrive.

Unfortunately, I have found that most people use the language of "basic" needs to collectively describe the needs for safety and connection, leaving the remaining needs hanging, poorly or wholly unarticulated. Honoring this natural tendency, I offer additional organizing language to support the full articulation of the needs that emerge beyond the basics.

Maslow felt our highest needs shift survival motivation from an orientation of fitness toward wisdom. These needs—intimacy and purpose—are about being our most developed self, so I'll refer to them as our "being" needs. While Maslow considered esteem as a basic need, I have found esteem more intermingles with the need for exploration. Together, they bridge the basic needs to the being needs. Therefore, esteem and exploration will be referred to as the "becoming" needs that unite the basic needs of safety and connection to the being needs of intimacy and purpose.

Basic needs. Basic needs reflect our innate motivation to physically and psychologically survive. Our body's essential anatomy and physiology as well as its demands of air, fuel, water, shelter, and sleep define our need for **safety**.

Loss of any one of these leads to death in short order. To forgo tending to the need for safety, the base of human development, is tantamount to building a house without a foundation. **Connection** is essential to flourishing, as we are evolutionarily determined social creatures. Developmentally, humans remain dependent longer than any other mammal. We require prolonged support from a community of others to adequately develop the rudimentary equipment needed to survive and thrive in the world. This initial support community carves the key neurobiological networks of our brain, and here we first learn how to connect to the world, others, and ourselves.

Becoming needs. When adequately satisfied, the basic needs open to becoming needs. Motivation begins a transition from a focus on deficiency and surviving to one of growth and thriving. Following the adequate satisfaction of safety and connection, the need for **esteem** emerges. Esteem is essential to move along the developmental continuum from dependence to independence. Our esteem encompasses the genetics and epigenetics that give rise to our unique constitutions, personalities, and capacities. As the need for **exploration** comes to bear, we exercise these capacities to learn our value in the world and the strength of agency, the ability to affect change. Satisfaction of becoming needs move us to a place where we ask "What choices will lead me to greater integration and wholeness?" rather than "How can I defend myself so that I can feel safe and secure?"[3]

Being needs. When the need for **intimacy** opens, the possibilities of true interdependence arise, orienting us to a prosocial understanding of the world. We are able to enter into intimate relationships to demonstrate and experience the beauty of compassion, especially self-compassion. Peak experiences and a deep sense of self-awareness harken the need for **purpose**. Wisdom and a stabilization of awareness beyond the self then provide the grounds for actualization and transcendence.

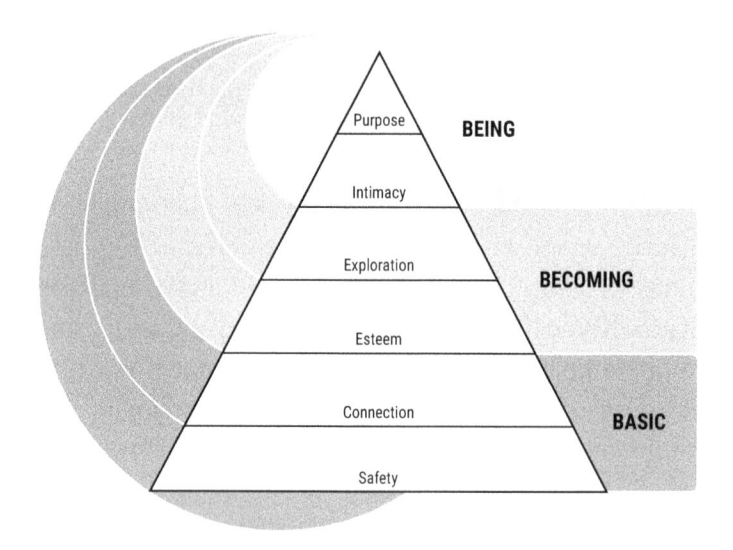

```
         Purpose       BEING
        Intimacy
       Exploration     BECOMING
         Esteem
       Connection      BASIC
          Safety
```

SUFFERING AND SELF-ACTUALIZATION
Suffering ends when we stop fearing things that we can't avoid.
— PAULO COELHO, THE ALCHEMIST

Suffering, approached from the lens of need satisfaction, gives a fresh context and significance to Maslow's renowned hierarchy. First, as I see it, needs are expressions of the fundamental laws of our existence and are the ultimate motivating force for optimal development:

Mortality, knowing one day we will die, underpins the need for safety.

Duality, the inherent oppositions required for anything to exist, reflects our need for connection.

Change, the child of time and space, manifests as the need for esteem.

Paradox, the consequence of duality coupled with change, harkens the need for exploration.

Interconnectivity, the inherent intermingling of all things, signals the need for intimacy.

Creativity, humanity's great calling, is expressed in our need for purpose.

For optimal evolution, these laws and their reflective needs are nonnegotiables. As Maslow believed, we are primarily motivated by dissatisfaction, and each of our needs, when unsatisfied, is "associated with its own distinct worldview."[4]

According to Maslow, needs are like a series of concentric circles, one embedded in the other. He goes on to describe this embeddedness as "needs [arranging] themselves in hierarchies of prepotency. That is to say, the appearance of one need usually rests on the prior satisfaction of another, more prepotent need."[5]

To simply demonstrate, the need for physical safety is represented by the largest circle and is the most "prepotent" need on which all other needs rest. As we grow and the prepotency of needs are sufficiently met, the other more nuanced needs open to support our developmental trajectory. Maslow called this opening of a new need as *emergence*:

> *"As for the concept of emergence of a new need after satisfaction of the prepotent need, this emergence is not a sudden, saltatory phenomenon but rather a gradual emergence by slow degrees from nothingness. For instance, if prepotent need A is satisfied only 10 percent, then need B may not be visible at all. However, as this need A becomes satisfied 25 percent, need B may emerge 5 percent, as need A becomes satisfied 75 percent, need B may emerge 50 percent, and so on."*[6]

These characteristics of prepotent embeddedness and gradual emergence create the strife we seemingly feel as we develop. It feels like we are constantly taking two steps forward and one step back. Remember adolescence? This herky-jerky feeling typically eases as we mature, in that we build what Maslow describes as *frustration tolerance,* wherein someone who experienced a prior satisfaction of a need is more tolerant to the future suffering of that need going unmet.[7] Regardless of the course, when needs emerge and are adequately satisfied, we develop. Our experiences can support this development or frustrate it, and at any given time or in any various context, all needs are signaling for our attention.

Second, while we are able to attend to multiple needs simultaneously, it has been my experience that the more personal, intimate aspect of suffering typically reflects our most unmet prepotent need. Quoting Maslow again:

> *"Everyday conscious desires are to be regarded as symptoms, as surface indicators of more basic needs. If we were to take these superficial desires at their face value, we would find ourselves in a state of complete confusion that could never be resolved, since we would be dealing seriously with symptoms rather than with what lay behind the symptoms."*[8]

And, as Kaufman states, "the greater the deficiency of these needs, the more we distort reality to fit our expectations and treat others in accordance with their usefulness in helping us satisfy our most deficient [need]."[9]

In caring for seriously ill patients across various settings and populations, I have come to see these distinct world views of unmet needs manifest as consistent yet personal patterns of suffering. Each time I sit at the bedside, I am awestruck by the clarity that a new diagnosis or prognosis can bring to a person's life. When the noise of everyday existence vanishes for those few moments, patients and their families reveal what matters most and, with it, a personal suffering that often accompanies the experience of this new information and its potentiality of threat.

Most commonly, the first pattern of suffering, *fear*, presents itself when one is confronted with one's own mortality and the threat of safety. However, fear is, sadly, frequently coupled with the suffering of *shame*. In an attempt to find some reason or sense of connection and control, people often assume they somehow are to blame or are deserved, forcing the tension found in the dualities that form the basis of human experience.

I also bear witness to the grief and loss that come from the inevitability of change and our willful *ignorance* to deny it. This is further compounded by complexities of paradox and the suffering of *judgment,* the most common response of having to hold two conflicting truths simultaneously. Further, the intimacies of interconnectivity of all things can elicit *isolation* when the smallness of life is so evident, and the wavelike power of creativity frequently leaves us suffering, *longing,* in its wakes of ebbs and flows.

The triangular relationship of evolutionary laws, human needs, and the patterns of suffering appear to have carved deep neural pathways of great evolutionary benefit. The scientific, philosophical, and religious traditions seemingly agree on this too, as the myths, parables, and archetypes all point to these foundational elements of our world and their promise of fulfillment.

Using these patterns of suffering—*fear, shame, ignorance, judgment, isolation,* and *longing*—afforded me the more nuanced language to bravely name the unwanted, uncontrollable, and unbearable aspects of life and offered me a rudimentary diagnostic pathway to support those living amid an individuated expression of suffering. By further naming suffering with these more shared and tangible human phenomena, people are often able to muster the courage to step toward, accept, and harness the power of suffering to shape their lives by simply (though not easily) beginning with meeting their most unmet need.

Additionally, the satisfactions of needs—*stability, belonging, knowledge, curiosity, compassion, and wisdom*—seem to round out each of the distinct worldviews, serving as a form of wayfinding along our developmental path. If the satisfaction of needs provides destination points on the map of our lives, then suffering is the compass by which we navigate.

Through the following sections of the book, we will explore the sufferings as they pertain to the developmental road map of fulfillment and actualization. Suffering adds dimensionality and movement to the hierarchy of prepotency as it initiates an upward spiraling cycle of need satisfaction that travels through the processes of suffering, choosing, creating, and dying. More specifically, opening with a deeper dive into each need, we'll follow with how we suffer when those needs are unmet, what elements of choice-making we can use to address those needs and create the context for the faculties of maturity to arise, and as those needs are satisfied, how our former selves die to our next becoming.

We start with the *sufferings of survival*: fear and shame. Reflecting the unmet basic needs of safety and connection, the sufferings of survival are the necessary motivators for fostering our early maturity in the faculties of attention and attachment. Bolstered by the skills of prediction and pause, we begin the developmental path with the stage of dependence marked by the basic satisfactions of stability and belonging.

As the basic survival needs are sufficiently satisfied, the becoming needs—esteem and exploration—emerge, and

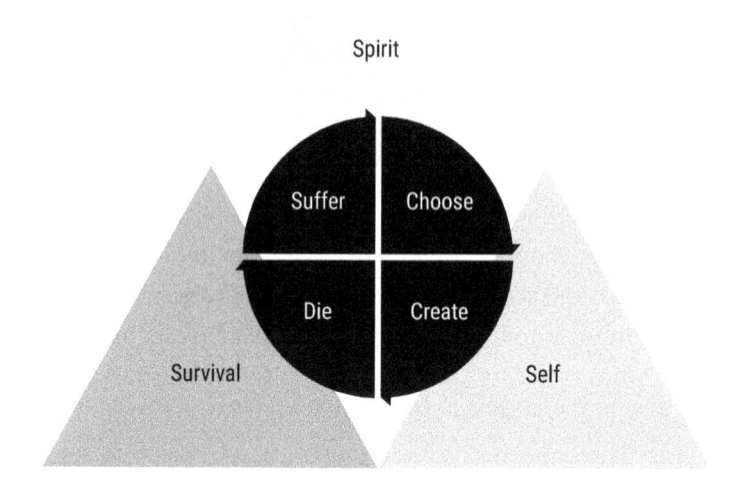

Compass of Suffering

we must navigate through ignorance and judgment, *the sufferings of self*, to bring about the satisfactions of knowledge and curiosity. Our development, further shaped by gaining perspective and holding paradox, then moves toward independence and the faculties of agency and aspiration.

Independence moves to interdependence, as our sense of self is adequately formed, and the faculties of acceptance and awareness unfold. The being needs of intimacy and purpose arise, and we suffer isolation and longing, the *sufferings of the spirit*. By choosing perseverance and passion, motivation aims to the satisfactions of compassion and wisdom, allowing for the blossoming of actualization and the final stage of development, transcendence.

While science is one of the languages used to explore the phenomenon of suffering, by no means are these observations evidenced, exhaustive, or conclusive. Gleaned over my years as a physician and healer, these offerings are meant to be a guided reflection rather than specific instruction, as suffering is so very personal. My wish is to make present the words that afford you the courage to take the first step toward your suffering. As Elie Wiesel, beloved author and Holocaust survivor, reminds us, "Suffering confers neither privileges nor rights; it all depends on how one uses it. If you use it to increase the anguish of yourself or others, you are degrading, even betraying it. Yet the day will come when we shall understand that suffering can elevate human beings. God help us to bear our suffering well."[10]

PART 2:

SUFFERING AND SATISFACTION OF NEEDS

Basic Needs and the Sufferings of Survival

...we can approach an understanding of...safety needs perhaps more efficiently by observation of infants and children, in whom these needs are much more simple and obvious. One reason for the clearer appearance of the threat or danger reaction in infants, is that they do not inhibit this reaction at all, whereas adults in our society have been taught to inhibit it at all costs.

—ABRAHAM MASLOW, *A THEORY OF HUMAN MOTIVATION*

Let's begin with a revisit to the human nervous system and its core relationship to basic needs and the sufferings of survival, fear and shame. As previously mentioned, our brain is organized by its three evolutionary parts: reptilian, mammalian, and human. Beginning with the reptilian part at its base, followed by the mammalian part, and topped with the human part, the organized hierarchy of the human brain looks like an upside-down layered cake.

Receiving the external world via our sensory system and internal information through its interoceptive capacities, the brain utilizes the mechanism of *sequential processing* in a bottom-up fashion that leads to the formation of experience and, ultimately, our behaviors and actions.[1]

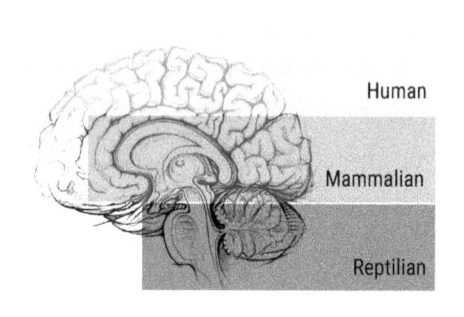

Sequential Processing

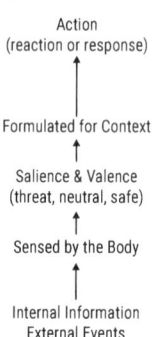

Human — Action (reaction or response)
↑
Formulated for Context
↑
Mammalian — Salience & Valence (threat, neutral, safe)
↑
Sensed by the Body
↑
Reptilian — Internal Information / External Events

The first step in sequential processing starts with the rudimentary, reptilian brain and its primal focus of survival. The survival bias comes from the implication of our mortality. We must live with the knowledge that one day we will die. This survival bias is created by the instinctive circuitry originating from our oldest brain. If sensory data or bits of internal information are perceived as a threat to our immediate survival or physical safety, we react with the immediacy of instinct. If no survival threat is sensed, things will move upward for continued processing.[2]

The mammalian brain receives the signals next, and its first response is to maintain homeostasis relative to our environment and activity. We are open systems, and homeostasis is the evolutionary mechanism that allows us to effectively respond to the universal conditions of our environment. This includes things like blood pressure, temperature, immunity, hunger, thirst, and fatigue. The mammalian brain also equips us with the hormones and neurotransmitters that formulate the drives of desire to address the dissatisfactions of our needs.

As creatures, we must perpetually manage the tensions in a multitude of contrasting dualities that together give rise to experience—light and dark, threat and safety, pain and pleasure. Like the rudimentary brain's survival bias, the mammalian brain has a negativity bias and is constantly scanning for sources of potential disruption, binarily categorizing everything in its path. On constant alert for things that might negatively impact our homeostasis, the mammalian brain works on impulse to steer our organism to not only avoid and relieve pain but to bask in the satisfaction of pleasure.

The middle brain's secondary function, the limbic system, further modifies the primal physiologic responses of the brainstem and the homeostatic responses of the middle brain. Now mind you (pun totally intended), we have minimal to no awareness of this experience yet. The limbic system is where our memories are stored and is the home of our psychological reflexes like feeling and emotion. To mitigate the constant flow of data, the middle brain functions like a prediction machine, creating habits and beliefs about the world. Consequently, our middle brain, without our conscious input, continues the chain reaction to protect our safety and security, and it responds with impulsive acts based on the predictive models it has manufactured.[3]

If the input poses no unmanageable threat and is deemed important enough to require the processing of executive function in the neocortex, we develop a conscious experience that is unique to the human brain. Only here can we comprehend, interpret, and choose an adjudicated response to the event or information being processed and act based on personal values and ethics.

Just think about the last time someone cut you off in traffic. What did you do? Perhaps you instinctively slammed on the brakes and then let out an impulsive rant of shouts and hand gestures, expressing your emotions of fear and anger, most of which you only became aware of after the fact. Or perhaps you purposefully averted the accident with minimal emotive load and continued to travel on your way.

Very simply put, we sense and receive external events and internal information. Then we draw attention by salience, determine valence, formulate context, and take action. Again, suffering occurs in the salience-valence-context process. While the instinctive and impulsive aspects of our brain can effectively manage and react to most of the input to our system, sequential processing can be compromised if our prediction machine is based on a skewed version of how safe we understand the world to be.

We are social creatures, and the primal safety and security networks of our brain and our beliefs about the world's safety are essentially laid down in parallel to the quality of secure dependency our first caregivers offered. With the longest childhood of all mammals, we humans are dependent upon others to lend us their safety and assist us in maintaining the stability of homeostasis. The suffering and satisfaction of the basic needs, safety and connection, consequently go hand-in-hand.

We learn early in development that "inclusion is the key to survival."[4] As outlined by violence expert Gavin de Becker in his acclaimed work, *The Gift of Fear*, inclusion is based on several essential rules of behavior that demonstrate how the sufferings of fear and shame are inextricably linked:

- We seek a degree of control over our lives.
- We will do more to avoid pain than we will to seek pleasure.
- We are saddened by loss and try to avoid it.
- We seek connection with others:
    – We care what others think of us.
    – We are "allergic" to rejection.
    – We seek significance in recognition and attention (even when it is negative).
    – We dislike ridicule and embarrassment.[5]

Further on this point, the groundbreaking CDC-Kaiser Permanente study on adverse childhood experiences (ACEs) clearly demonstrates how significantly early childhood shapes the way we develop and ultimately experience the world on a day-to-day basis. Substantiating the correlation between childhood adversity and the development of health risk behavior and chronic illness, the study inarguably demonstrates the importance of how the adequate satisfaction of our basic needs and the consequential necessities of stability and belonging are fundamental to our successful development as humans.[6]

To this end, Maslow's theory, controversially, was both significantly influenced and challenged by his work with the Blackfoot People of the Siksika reserve. In the summer of 1938, Maslow immersed himself in the Blackfoot society where "self-actualization was the norm."[7] Recent research and reflections by First Nation social scientists suggest that "Maslow saw self-actualization as something to earn," where, as best summarized by social entrepreneur Teju Ravilochan in his article entitled "The Blackfoot Wisdom that Inspired Maslow's Hierarchy":

> "...the Blackfoot see [self-actualization] as innate. Relating to people as inherently wise involves trusting them and granting them space *to express who they are*...rather than *making them* the best they can be. For many First Nations, therefore, self-actualization is not achieved; it is drawn out of an inherently sacred being who is imbued with a spark of divinity."[8]

Ravilochan goes on to state that "many First Nation cultures see the work of meeting basic needs, ensuring safety, and creating conditions for the expression of purpose as a community responsibility, not an individual one...creating a culture of generosity, trust, and cooperation, rather than one of inequality and individualism."[9]

Toward the end of his life, Maslow recognized his misperception on individualism, as his own self-critique of the hierarchy theory emphasizes that "personal salvation cannot be really understood in isolation...it is quite clear that...individualist psychology without reference to other people and social conditions is not adequate."[10] Maslow's writing suggests he came to believe that the primary responsibility of caregivers like parents, teachers, therapists, and clinicians is to "enable people to become healthy and effective in their own style."[11]

Humanistic psychologist Scott Barry Kaufman eloquently summarized this amended view as: "It was [Maslow's] belief that if society can create the conditions to satisfy one's basic needs—including the freedom to speak honestly and openly, to grow and develop one's unique capacities and passions, and to live in a society with fairness and justice—what naturally and organically emerges tends to be the characteristics that resemble the *best* in humanity."[12]

Illustrating the importance of a safe, connected community and its lacking in modern-day American society—seemingly worse now than in Maslow's time—many of the patients I have treated seem stuck in a state of chronically unmet survival needs. This often results in widespread experiences of fear and shame, manifesting as insecurities, codependence, and underdeveloped senses of self. The wellness industry, in an informal yet highly influential partnership with the healthcare industry, unthinkingly encourages people to bypass tending to their basic needs in favor of promise, passion, and purpose. On this point, social critic Ruth Whippman writes in her poignant article entitled, "Where Were We While the Pyramid Was Collapsing? At a Yoga Class":

> "We have developed a new and pervasive cultural narrative around human well-being that has seeped through virtually all sections of society. This narrative inverts Maslow's pyramid, positing self-realization not just as something to pursue when

the basic fundamentals are in place, but as a viable alternative to those fundamentals.... Rather than seeing psychological health and flourishing as the result of a basic social contract that aims to provide for all, we are increasingly seeing it as the result of individual effort, divorced from our circumstances or the societies in which we live.... We are focusing on the tip of Maslow's pyramid at the clear expense of its base."[13]

Our experiences and narratives about the past formulate the basis of our brain's predictive processing and reactivity. The societal norm of "bootstrap" individuality, reinforced by our experienced degrees of safety and community, sets up neglect, trauma and other overwhelming emotional experiences to have the propensity for creating hypervigilant lower and middle brains, resulting in the sufferings of fear and shame.

These exposed brain centers quickly learn to react to the slightest threat instinctively or impulsively, and when we perceive and predict the world through a lens of hypervigilance, we operate from preprogrammed reactions of survival. Once self-preserving, these ongoing reactions to the events of our past may no longer be of service as they may briefly relieve the pain of an unmet basic need in the present at the cost of its long-term satisfaction in the future, and the cycle of suffering is perpetuated.

In one of the most poignant discussions of satisfying basic needs to break the cycle of sufferings rooted in survival, Oprah Winfrey in collaboration with Dr. Bruce Perry, a world-renowned pediatric psychiatrist, provides hope in their book entitled *What Happened to You?* Through storytelling and conversation, Winfrey and Perry sensitively illustrate the brilliant resiliency of the brain, especially its survival ability in responding to trauma as well as its capacity to heal and rewire:

> "Once we know the source of the problem, we can better understand how to fix it. In a sequence that replicates the original construction of the house—the brain—we put in place a 'rebuilding/renovation plan.' With the problem areas in mind, we can provide experiences—both educational and therapeutic—that jump-start and reorganize the systems that were impacted by neglect, adversity, and trauma."[14]

Perry and Winfrey go on to say:

> "Adversity, challenges, disappointment, loss and trauma—all can contribute to the capacity to be broadly empathetic, and become wise…[but] the cost of wisdom can be very high. And for many people, the pain never goes away. The wise learn how to carry their burden with grace, often to protect others from the emotional intensity of their pain."

Transforming the sufferings of survival is shaped by the mantra of their book:

> "Without some degree of regulation, it is difficult to connect with another person, and without connection, there is minimal reasoning.… We must first regulate to relate, and only then can we reason."[15]

Armed with the understanding of basic needs and their origins in sequential processing and social inclusion, we are now ready to navigate the in-depth discussions of the sufferings of fear and shame, the practices of prediction and pause, the faculties of attention and attachment, and satisfactions of stability and belonging.

Fear.

Fear is always there within us—the fear of getting old, the fear of getting sick, the fear of dying, the fear of being abandoned by our loved ones. It is very human to be fearful and to worry about it... Every time your fear is invited up, every time you recognize it and smile at it, your fear will lose some of its strength.

—THICH NHAT HAHN, *NO DEATH, NO FEAR*

SAFETY: AM I SAFE?
Since fear is so central to our experience, understanding when it is a gift—and when it is a curse—is well worth the effort... Whether it is learned the easy way or the hard way, the truth remains your safety is yours.

—GAVIN DE BECKER, *THE GIFT OF FEAR*

Two instances in my early young adulthood solidified my appreciation of fear and its capacity to guide my life. First, as an emergency room volunteer, when medical school was still a dream, I was making rounds to provide coffee and water to family members sitting vigil while their loved ones received the emergency care they needed. Turning the corner to the hall where the most concerning cases were treated, I felt premonitory fear lick up my spine.

Just seconds later, I instinctively turned to see a gurney holding a patient receiving CPR crash through the door into the hallway that moments before was quietly holding the murmurings of help and healing. Swept into the melee, I finally settled at the bay door standing hand-in-hand with a woman where the sequence of lifesaving procedures continued to march forward in an effort to save her husband, and gobsmacked, I watched death unfold. While I didn't know it at the time, this dance between fear and death would become my life's work.

Second, while a medical student, I sustained an episode of anaphylaxis, a severe allergic reaction where the body launches into full defense mode to dispel a threatening substance that has found its way into your body. About halfway through my daily four-mile run, I suddenly sneezed. Having righted myself, after nearly faceplanting on the treadmill, I succumbed to a torrent of continued sneezing, a raging river of snot, profuse sweating and swelling, tears, stomach cramping, and painful full-body tingling.

Fear flooded my system and released a rush of adrenaline propelling me like a magnetized force toward a source of help and safety. By the graces, several of my classmates were close by and got me to the emergency room. In short order, I began to wheeze and couldn't find my breath. In a last-ditch effort to preserve itself, my body was closing the last potential source of entry for its perceived poison—my airway.

The memories I have of those last moments before I passed out seem disjointed and distant, like watching a movie of my life rather than actually living it. Mercifully, antihistamines and steroids quickly reversed the process, and I eventually returned to my body. In the aftermath, I now know: 1) to take care not to expose myself to excessive heat or strain after eating and 2) fear saved my life.

In these encounters, I discovered a vital lesson. Fear is a valuable gift, a "potent ally" whose summons should never be ignored.[1]

Fear sits at the foundation of all suffering, eliciting its universal qualities of unwantedness, uncontrollability, and unbearableness. With our mortality on the line, survival instincts drive routine behaviors. Only with the regulation of stability found in the satisfaction of safety can we begin to relate and make meaningful connections. The suffering of fear is so intense because of the essential needs it stands to represent. Rightly so, as safety is the most prepotent need. Quoting Maslow, "…for our chronically and extremely hungry man, Utopia can be defined very simply as a place where there is plenty of food."[2] With our self-preserving instincts fueled by the power of fear, we are preprogrammed for survival.

Fear is a recognition of the fundamental truth that one day we will die. The inevitability of death sits at the backdrop of our day-to-day lives, regardless of circumstances. If we lose our breath, our death will come in seconds; if we are exposed to the extremes of illness and environment (including other people and predators), minutes; loss of water and food equates to a loss of life in days; and finally, no sleep indolently robs us of life in a matter of weeks. Underpinning all other sufferings, the suffering of fear reminds us of our fragility, impermanence, and our "creatureliness."[3]

At the heart of his Pulitzer Prize-winning book, *The Denial of Death,* author and cultural anthropologist Ernest Becker delves into this creatureliness, its need for safety and unrelenting calls of fear. He writes "…the fear of death is universal…it is the basic fear that influences all others, a fear from which no one is immune, no matter how disguised it may be…who wants to face up fully to the creatures that we are, clawing and gasping for breath in a universe beyond our ken?"[4]

Fear is also a controversial topic.[5] Heavily debated in psychology and neuroscience, fear has been described as a state, an emotion, a feeling, a circuit, a reflex, a process, and more. Focusing on fear as an experience of suffering, it is "urgent…triggered in the present moment in response to [a] known, definite, and immediate threat."[6] "Fear is [also] involuntary…fear occurs in the presence of danger and will always easily link to pain or death."[7] Until the frontiers of science redefine our conceptualization of death, we must live under this rule of survival in an appreciation of our creatureliness. Overtly and subtly, the suffering of fear, though rooted in death and dying, is essential to life and living.

In context, fear is a normal aspect of our spectrum of wakefulness that stretches from calm, through alert and alarm, to fear and fear's extreme form, terror.[8] Reflective of sequential processing, the spectrum sits in parallel to the brain structures and functions responsible for perceiving threats. Human intuition and cognition is accessible in the wakeful states of calm and alert, mammalian impulses take over when in perceptions of alarm, and our rudimentary reptilian instincts kick in with fear and terror. Additionally, adapted for survival, evolution has equipped us with two primary mechanisms for responding to the perceived threats—one of arousal and the other of dissociation. As poignantly articulated by Dr. Bruce Perry, pediatric psychiatrist and trauma specialist:

> "In the arousal response…to prepare for fight or flight, our heart rate increases; adrenaline and related stress hormones like cortisol are released, as is sugar stored in our muscles; blood is diverted to our muscles. The general focus of the response is external."[9]

He continues with a corresponding discussion of dissociation:

> "Dissociation is a complex mental capability that we use in everyday life…the dissociative response is a continuum…[it] helps us rest, replenish, survive injury and tolerate pain. Where arousal sends blood to the muscles, dissociation keeps blood in the trunk to minimize blood loss in case of injury…dissociation releases the body's own pain killers."[10]

Consequently, fear can overtly manifest in two basic forms. In its arousal form, fear is fueled by the primal emotion of rage manifesting the instincts of aggression and violence. Dissociated, fear merges with anguish, exhibiting the instinctual behavior of feigning death. There is no choice in which of the two mechanisms our instinctual brain will use to react to a perceived threat. We can only be aware of these capacities to better equip ourselves to heed the call of fear in whichever form it takes.

Arousal Fear Response (Rage)

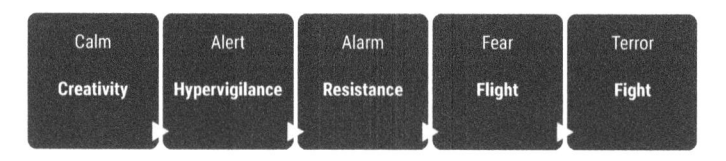

Calm	Alert	Alarm	Fear	Terror
Creativity	Hypervigilance	Resistance	Flight	Fight

Arousal Fear Response: As most people can articulate, we have the "fight or flight" arousal response. This spectrum of arousal reaction stretches from a calm reflective state related to creativity to a state of terror that reigns with rage-fueled aggression and violence.[11]

Dissociative Fear Response (Anguish)

Calm	Alert	Alarm	Fear	Terror
Daydreaming	Avoidance	Compliance	Dissociation	Collapse

Dissociative Fear Response: The dissociative pathway is frequently seen in the animal world (a.k.a. "playing possum") and is now being more appreciated in the human world. The dissociative response kicks in when the system believes its options for arousal are futile and prepares itself to take on pain, loss, and potential death. Mitigated by the body's natural opioid system and the collapsing emotion of anguish, fear results in worst cases with paralysis or unconsciousness.[12]

In our modern day, we rarely experience fear so overtly. Subtly, fear mostly shows up in the uncertainty of basic necessities. When living with a chronically unmet need for safety, for many, scarcity becomes a way of life. We need clean air to breathe. We need food for fuel. Water is essential for…everything. Shelter protects us from the extremes so that each night we can safely lay our head down for the necessary sleep our minds and bodies need to survive. Yet so many people are living without basic food, water, shelter, and consequently, sleep.

As demonstrated by the work Maslow did with the Blackfoot Nation, the culture and abundance of a society to successfully shape the satisfaction of these basics is directly reflected in its members' longevity and actualization. Failure to meet the basic necessities leads to the severe consequences of violence and premature death, as polluted air, food insecurity, chronic dehydration, ill-defined illnesses, inaccessible healthcare, financial instability and widespread poverty, ignored domestic violence, persistent war, and rewarded exhaustion all rob us of our humanity.

As an American physician, I am still shocked to see so many patients living with chronically unmet safety needs.

In the phenomenon that I call *the scarcity of more,* relatively affluent societies, like the US, who also experience significant disparities between those who have too little and those who have too much, seem to have very few members actually getting their basic safety needs met.

Social epidemiologist Richard Wilkinson demonstrated—using a broad range of health metrics including life expectancy, obesity, trust, mental illness, violence, and social mobility—that economic inequality predicts the health of a nation. Wilkinson persuasively argues this point in his much-viewed 2011 TED Talk:

> "…inequality is divisive and socially corrosive…the average well-being of our societies is not dependent any longer on national income and economic growth… Kids do worse in the more unequal societies… the big change in our understanding of drivers of chronic health in the rich developed world is how important chronic stress from social sources is affecting the immune system, the cardiovascular system. Or for instance, the reason why violence becomes more common in more unequal societies is because people are sensitive to being looked down on."
>
> To reinforce the point, Wilkinson mischievously adds, "If Americans want to live the American dream, they should go to Denmark."[13]

Further illustrating the scarcity of more, psychologists Adam Grant and Barry Schwartz penned a controversial article entitled "Too Much of a Good Thing: The Challenge and

Opportunity of the Inverted U." In it they state, "There is no such thing as an unmitigated good. All positive traits, states, and experiences have costs that at high levels may begin to outweigh their benefits, creating the non-monotonicity of an inverted U."[14] Non-monotonicity is the point where the "good" thing hits the inflection point and becomes "bad."

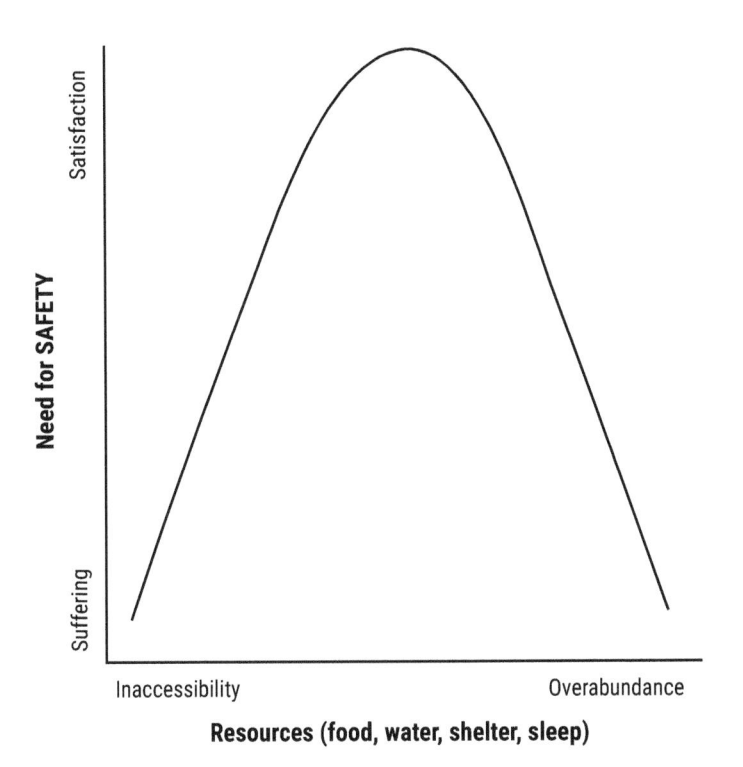

[Graph: An inverted U curve. Y-axis labeled "Need for SAFETY" ranging from "Suffering" (bottom) to "Satisfaction" (top). X-axis labeled "Resources (food, water, shelter, sleep)" ranging from "Inaccessibility" to "Overabundance".]

Taking a similar approach of its use in many domains of psychology, the application of the Inverted U to resources relative to the suffering and satisfaction of basic needs—air, water, fuel, shelter, sleep—appears to play out in the minute-to-minute actions of our daily lives, demonstrating that at the extremes of inequality—inaccessibility and overabundance—the ability to meet our basic needs is severely compromised and suffering prevails.

Food security exemplifies these two faces of the inverted U with the inequality of inaccessibility at one end and overabundance on the other. Inaccessibility is painfully simple, where there is no food—ranging from famine to food deserts—too many people live hungry and starving. The statistics are staggering: forty-four million people in the US, including thirteen million children, live with food insecurity; in recent years, nearly forty-nine million used food programs; and 100 percent of US counties have food insecurity.[15]

This crisis is coupled with the other inequity extreme of food overabundance, a more complicated and duplicitous issue. The food industry has infiltrated our food supply with processed goods empowered with hyperpalatable chemistry that "co-opt" our survival circuitry.[16] These enticing food stuffs are not only abundant, but they are readily available at all hours, require little work to obtain, and cost multiples less than the food we actually need to fuel our bodies.

Addiction to these "legal" substances is rampant, and hunger cues are now replaced with sugar cravings that are experienced like those of cocaine.[17] The "food rules" industry has overzealously sprung up as an antithesis, and now disordered eating has become the backdrop of our meals. In overabundance, food for fuel gets lost in fake-cheap foodstuff, food for entertainment, food rules, or food for emotional soothing. Suffering the fear of no food seemingly shifts from a quantitative experience to a qualitative one.

These extremes of food access, not enough and too much, greatly challenge our ability to make food choices best suited to meet our basic need for fuel. When I shared this concept with a colleague, they heartachingly reflected on this idea and offered:

> "Fear is fundamental, so it is apolitical, genderless, and universal. Fear is such a primal concept that is relatable and can keep people stuck in a perpetual loop of stress. Keeping people in fear is one of the ways the masses are kept in control and is played out every day in America. Governments reject proposals to end food deserts, relocate unhoused individuals to inhospitable areas, increase restrictions and requirements for assistance, fail to protect the food chain, and much more in the simple pursuit of keeping people hungry."

Water, similarly, is either inaccessible or polluted on one side or lost to the cesspool of plastic bottles, energy drinks, and sugar laden cocktails on the other. While not clearly demonstrated in the medical literature, public statistics claim that upward of 75 percent of Americans are chronically dehydrated.[18] In my experience, personally and professionally, dehydration underpins our daily "blah" feeling and significantly contributes to the sequelae of serious illness. Chronic dehydration has become normal, thirst unrecognizable, leaving our brains screaming for the simplicity of water.

Our brains are also screaming for sleep, as evidenced by the facts that one in three US adults report not getting enough rest or the concerning estimate that fifty to seventy million

Americans have chronic, or ongoing, sleep disorders.[19] Sleep's inverted U can be shaped by numerous things—work hours, parenting, or even hormones. However, I see the environment where we lay our head down to sleep as the key resource to meeting this basic need. Our bodies require the various stages of sleep to undergo its necessary restoration and repair, and we are highly vulnerable in the paralytics of deep sleep.

On the extreme where safety resources are scarce, the environment is often infused with the threat of domestic violence. With no safe place to curl up, the body remains on the ready with cortisol and adrenaline. A nervous system on alert for safety doesn't receive the restorative sleep it desperately needs to function effectively. On the other extreme where sleep resources are aplenty, we see things like *revenge bedtime procrastination*—"the decision to sacrifice sleep for leisure time that is driven by a daily schedule lacking in free time"—compromising the need for sleep.[20]

Desperate to escape the frenetic nature of modern living, we doomscroll and binge-watch, filling the environment with stimulating blue light, flooding our nervous system with dopamine, and numbing the fear of tomorrow's schedule. The dysfunction that results from a loss of a few nights of sleep, whatever the cause, can be life-threatening, and as sleep scientist Dr. Matt Walker says, "The best bridge between despair and hope is a good night's sleep."[21]

Nowhere was the need for a safe environment more evident than during the pandemic. The pandemic revealed many things, but our need for shelter took center stage. All of us were collectively exposed to pathogens in a way we've not seen for a century or more, financial vulnerability lurked around each corner, and home, for many, became unsafe. Protection from the elements—weather, pestilence, microbes, animals (including other people)—was seemingly compromised in one fell swoop, rendering many in a mental state of fear-based "guns out" fight or flight living and, socially, we lost essential structure, order, law, and limits. Safety was found not in material resources but in the precious few people and places where our nervous system or our immune defenses weren't in DEFCON 1. The Inverted U of our social nature and its relationship to safety was revealed. Too many people is no good, too few isn't either, and protective, safe people and places are a rare a precious commodity that all of us require for our lives to be stable.

Recognizing that each of these topics deserve entire chapters of their own, for our discussion they are highlighted to demonstrate two things: 1) inequity breeds unnecessary suffering for all members of a community, especially when it comes to safety and 2) as a consequence, our body-minds don't know what is real anymore. The signals of our basic needs—hunger, thirst, fatigue, illness, fear—when left in perpetual alarm, fade to the background, unattended, and we unwittingly suffer.

PRACTICING PREDICTION

Fear is a kind of unintentional storytelling that we're all born knowing how to do. Our fears focus our attention on a question that is as important in life as it is in literature: what will happen next... How we choose to read our fears can have a profound effect on our lives.

— KAREN THOMPSON, *TED TALK ON FEAR*

Prediction is the developmental skill that transitions us from living in fear to effectively managing it. It marks the foundational step in fulfilling our need for safety and, consequently, all our other fundamental needs. Prediction forges a partnership with our instinctual capacities, setting the stage for our attention to emerge. Together, prediction and attention represent the transformative forces essential for addressing an unmet need of safety, alleviating the suffering of fear and leading us toward the satisfaction of stability.

Prediction first requires us to be present in our bodies. Sadly, we have seemingly forgotten that we are "feeling creatures that on occasion think," and we have lost confidence in our abilities to predict what needs are at risk.[22] "Fear is a signal intended to be very brief...unanswered fear is destructive, [yet] millions choose to stay there."[23] If "one feels fear...all the time, there is no signal reserved for the times when it's really needed,"[24] and our ability to predict becomes compromised, resulting in what pediatric psychiatrist Dr. Bruce Perry calls "functional vulnerability." Functional vulnerability represents the "cascade of risk in emotional, social, mental, and physical health" that leaves the residue of suffering.[25] It seems we don't trust our bodies.

Embodiment, recognizing how our body informs and shapes our experiences of the world, is something most of us must relearn. For a deep dive into this topic, I'll point you to the work of Drs. Antonio Damasio and Bessel van der Kolk, as they are both pioneers in Western science who recognize and study the importance of the body-mind connection to live a fully actualized life.[26]

Here, I'll mention Van der Kolk's seminal work, *The Body Keeps the Score*, where he plumbs the depths of what we know about harnessing the "brain's own natural neuroplasticity to help [trauma] survivors feel fully alive in the present…gain control over the residues of past trauma, and return to being masters of their own ship."[27] Van der Kolk emphasizes the importance of embodiment:

> "Talking, understanding, and human connections help, and drugs can dampen hyperactive alarm systems. But we…see that the imprints from the past can be transformed by having physical experiences that directly contradict the helplessness, rage, and collapse that are part of trauma, and thereby regaining self-mastery."[28]

We all have an imperative to first learn how to feel safe in our own bodies. Damasio, in his seminal work, *The Feeling of What Happens,* states, "Sometimes we use our minds not to discover facts, but to hide them. We use part of the mind as a screen to prevent another part of it from sensing what goes on elsewhere… One of the things the screen hides most effectively is the body, our own body, by which I mean the ins of it, its interiors. Like a veil thrown over the skin to secure

FEAR.

its modesty, the screen partially removes from the mind the inner states of the body, those that constitute the flow of life as it wanders in the journey of each day."[29]

Returning to Gavin de Becker, violence expert and protector of society's most important personalities, in *The Gift of Fear* he states, "Impulses are pre-incident indicators for action."[30] This concept of *pre-incident indicators* is the basis of prediction. De Becker outlines how his protection work is founded in systematizing pre-incident indicators to manage fear and predict safety in the context of fatal violence. In line with Van der Kolk's work, de Becker's best advice is "'listen to yourself': 1) when you feel fear, listen; 2) when you don't feel fear, don't manufacture it; 3) If you find yourself creating worry, explore and discover why."[31] This adage can easily extend to daily life:

1. *When you feel fear, listen.* As we discussed earlier, many of us experience fear in its more subtle forms of hunger, fatigue, thirst, and illness as a constant way of being. Even in our modern day, we still benefit from the instinctive survival system and its ability to alert us to clear and present danger. However, what constitutes clear and present danger in a savanna filled with strip malls, skyscrapers, and cellphones? "Context is everything," de Becker states, "…it is the necessary link that gives meaning to everything we observe, [yet] people are often reluctant to put it ahead of content…just as some people are quick to predict the worst, there are others who are reluctant to accept that they might actually be in some danger."[32] Denial and worry, consequences of a dulled sense of safety, cloud our abilities to appropriately feel our fear and use it.

2. *When you don't feel fear, don't manufacture it.* Denial, worry, and panic—what de Becker suggests are voluntary forms of "self-harassment"—only serve to unnecessarily further our suffering of the unmet need for safety. He goes on to say, "[practice] caution and precaution but avoid having it replace perception of what is actually happening with imaginings of what could happen."[33]
3. *If you find yourself creating worry, explore and discover why.* De Becker goes on to recognize that creating worry comes from uncertainty, a more subtle form of fear.[34] Hunger, thirst, fatigue, illness, and malaise—these are all pre-incident indicators to the impending compromise of safety and the suffering of fear. When you recognize worry, first contextualize the uncertainty by asking—"Am I safe?" Confirming there is no immediate threat, move through the steps to meeting your body's needs. Take a breath, get some water and food, rest, and reevaluate. Reminding us of Oprah's mantra, we must first regulate to relate to then reason.[35]

Prediction also requires preparation. Professionally, in medicine, we are indoctrinated to manage our fear. In advanced cardiovascular life support training, health professionals are drilled in protocols for treating the most common fatal cardiopulmonary events.[36] Gained through simulated mock code blues, repeated ad nauseum, we prepare our nervous systems, coaxing them into fear-tolerant, lifesaving machines. We also have an intense learning conference call M&M, short for morbidity and mortality. At M&M, we review patient stories and outcomes where there was an unexpected injury (morbidity) or death (mortality). Traditionally, at the postmortem, senior doctors publicly castigate young physicians on perceived errors and missteps, all in effort to instill the "fear of God" as to never make a mistake again. While these are extreme and barbaric learning processes and ones I do not recommend, they did teach me the value of repetition and hindsight as powerful ways to learn, prepare, and predict.

Every day when we create our daily schedule, we practice prediction through preparation. You choose what you will be exposed to, what risks will be involved, and how you will care for your body. Bookended with the postmortem, we can reflect on the day and take its lessons learned to prepare for the next, expanding our capacity to predict. When we learn to predict, less fear will abound, safety becomes satisfied, and we are able to grow.

"Predictability is what holds human societies together."[37] Undeniably, millions of people around the world live without the fundamental basics to survive, and closing the inequity gap is essential to improving the health of every member of society. We all require consistent, unconditional love and care throughout our lives but particularly during times of vulnerability, especially when we are young. Closing inequity gaps and ensuring that each of us has enough resources to be safe are lofty goals. Big changes start with small ones, and we are of no use to each other when we are walking through the world dysregulated or disassociated. So, it must start with you. Can you, in this moment, honor your suffering of fear, meet your need for safety, so that when called upon you can help someone else do the same?

ATTENTION

...like currency, attention can be paid, given, or stolen; it is extremely valuable, and also finite... Yet attention is not something that can be banked or borrowed. It cannot be saved to use later. We can only use our attention in the here and now... Pay attention like your life depends on it.

— DR. AMISHI JHA, NEUROSCIENTIST

As discussed previously, choices transform each suffering to create new faculties that then lead to need satisfaction. What I have come to call the faculties of maturity—*attention, attachment, agency, aspiration, acceptance, and awareness*—are conceptual experiences created in the context of their exercised developmental choices—*practicing prediction, invoking the pause, gaining perspective, holding paradox, committing to persevere, and playing passion*. While not a part of Maslow's theory, they do, in my experience, appear to be the basis for frustration tolerance, our ability to experience, recognize, and manage unmet needs.

Through sequential processing, external events and internal information frequently disrupt homeostasis and the satisfaction of our needs. Exercising the developmental choices creates the context for the faculties of maturity to arise. This coupling shifts homeostatic disruption from collapsing to motivating, building our tolerance to frustrated needs. With more frustration tolerance, we are better able to assess our circumstances, identify suffering, and move toward satisfaction to regain homeostatic happiness.

Following this logic, transforming the suffering of fear begins with practicing prediction, and prediction then creates the context for attention to arise. Our ability to practice prediction rudimentarily refines the processing of external and internal sensory data and allows us, as neuroscientist Dr. Amishi Jha says, "to pay attention to our attention." Attention is the "powerful, trainable, yet fragile" filter our brain develops to manage the onslaught of information it continuously receives through sequential processing.[38] Attention is the foundational faculty that affords us the ability to suffer well. Like the need for safety being prepotent to all other needs, attention appears to be prepotent to all other faculties.

William James, nineteenth-century philosopher whose influence remains strong even today, named this pairing of prediction and attention in his celebrated work entitled *The Principles of Psychology*. As summarized by Jamesian scholars, "When it comes to giving an account of the 'intimate nature of the attention process,' James [identifies] two fairly simple processes: a) The adjustment of the sensory organs (such processes as pointing one's ears in the right direction, bringing one's eyes into focus, taking a sniff, and so on), and b) anticipatory preparation (what James has in mind here is simply *imagination*. His claim is that when attention does not involve adjusting one's sense organs it consists in imagining the things or actions that one is attending to or looking for.)"[39] James verdantly claims:

"My experience is what I agree to attend to."[40]

Taking the first part of James's attention process, "the adjustment of sensory organs," we can routinely make it a point to aim our sight, hearing, smell, taste and touch.[41] Finding quiet moments throughout the day when we stop, get into the body, and shift to sensing, we exercise our attention through embodiment. By directing our "sensory organs" to listen and contextualize the body's cues of hunger, thirst, fatigue, stress, and illness, we may appropriately attend to the body's needs. Embodiment is not easy, yet it is essential to a fulfilling life. Paradoxically, we find a sense of aliveness in the discomfort of embodiment. We will further explore this relationship between sensations and associated feelings, emotions, affect, and mood in coming chapters.

From a place of focus and recognition of what is happening in the present moment, we then deploy James's second process of imagining. Here we perform the postmortem to free ourselves from the past and better equip us to imagine what is possible for the future. Our attentional capacities, honed by predictive practices, empower us to effectively manage threats to our safety and misfires of the threat response system. Especially when we experience an event that literally or proverbially "takes our breath away," evoking the suffering of fear, prediction and attention are the tools we use to transform its power.

Attention, like all the faculties of maturity, surfaces and must be stabilized. Sadly, modernity bombards us with information and sensory overload, shattering our attention with its constant demands. The stress of attentional demands sets off the cascade of threat, where we rapidly toggle between the adaptive arousal and dissociation mechanisms to the onslaught of data. We consequently begin to shift further down the wakefulness spectrum, depleting physical and cognitive resources while firing our lower brain functions, and we suffer.

In everyday life, persistent arousal states may make us look like someone who is edgy, critical, quick to jump to worst-case scenario, and chronic dissociative responses mirror withdraw, avoidance, or people pleasing. Furthermore, these experiences of hyperalertness cause us to frequently misperceive threats. These misfires beget further misfires, which leads to more dysregulation and overactive threat alarm.

attentional demand =
more dysregulation and instability =
less ability to relate and connect =
unsafe = fear = suffering

Our suffering reflects the dissonance between what we claim to value and what we actually attend to in our daily schedules. One of the most profound lessons the dying impart to the living is that in embracing the reality of death, you get really clear on what matters most, where you want to spend your time, and with whom. There is nothing like fear, particularly the fear of death, to call one's attention. In this overt fear, we gain an acute appreciation for life. So why do we wait for a crisis to attend to the things that matter most when there is more than enough suffering in the subtle day-to-day, when all our pre-incident indicators are there for us in the plain sight of our desk calendar?

Attention is essential for stability, the adequate satisfaction of the need for safety. Without it, our need for connection remains unopened to us. As mindfulness teacher Jack Kornfield states, "With inattention, we miss the meal in front of us, the parade of passerby, the ever-changing scenery, the openhearted connection with the world."[42]

STABILITY

Maslow argued that everything that is "nasty, mean, or vicious" is an overcompensatory attempt to satisfy the basic needs… the base upon which all other [needs] are fulfilled… In the absence of that base, people become overly dependent…which can compromise growth, development, and meaning in life.
— SCOTT BARRY KAUFMAN, *TRANSCEND*

Maslow describes the satisfaction of our safety need as "security; stability; dependence; protection; freedom from fear, from anxiety and chaos."[43] With a bias to survival, our instinctive circuitry attempts to rectify any dissonance between safety and threat. When dissonance leads to dissatisfaction, we are motivated to seek its relief. If left unchecked, we suffer fear. Rooted in our most primitive brains, fear uses our stress response system to act from levels of instinct and impulse to keep the body alive. When fear arises, we must honor its call and immediately attend to the emergent threat. However, when fear moves beyond its brief, urgent nature into a more indolent, chronic form of uncertainty or stress, we must choose to transform it or be perpetually subjected to suffering.

Fear is transformed by the practice of prediction and the development of attention. When coupled effectively, they move us from the suffering of fear to the satisfaction of stability. With the need for safety adequately addressed, the need for connection arises.

Connection

Safety

Fear | Prediction

Stability | Attention

Basic stability is the fertile ground from which blossoming human development must take root. From the prepotent power of stability, we are able to reclaim our attention and open our eyes to life beyond threat.

I assume if you are reading this, your safety needs are adequately met enough in this moment to allow you the choice to crack open a book. The irony is not lost. However, there has probably been a time when you experienced fear and suffering, and there will likely be another. Someone close to you is probably experiencing fear and suffering. Regardless, your time and attention are being called. Are you prepared?

Shame.

Shame is the intensely painful feeling...that washes over us, making us feel small, flawed, never good enough, and therefore unworthy of...belonging and connection.
—BRENÉ BROWN, *THE GIFTS OF IMPERFECTION*

Just under five feet tall with gleaming crystal-blue eyes and a wicked smile, Jo was a tenacious, spry gem of a human. When she arrived at Clarehouse, the home for dying people where I am a member of a caring team dedicated to the development of a death-aware community, Jo was in a tumultuous relationship with cancer. Her eyes flashed with a cool resentment, and her dry humor had an undeniable bite. The cancer had been diagnosed just a handful of months prior, and despite the arduous regimen of chemotherapy and radiation that Jo and her family had faithfully upheld, it had continued to spread like wildfire through her body. Her first words to me, through gritted teeth and pursed lips, were, "I am not afraid of death."

My response was, "I hear you. How do feel about dying?"

With a "*harrumph*," she turned her gaze to the ceiling, ending the conversation.

Over the weeks we cared for her, Jo softened…a little. In the week before her death, I opened Jo's door for a visit, only to be impaled by a gaze so full of emotion that it stopped me in my tracks, causing me to reach for my abdomen to make sure it was still intact. Closing the door, I took a deep breath, settled at her bedside, and watched Jo finally lean into her suffering. Along with her tears, shame flooded the room. Shame for being more than a woman of her generation was allowed, shame for the young woman who was less than "ladylike," shame for living as a wife in title only, shame that though she loved her children, she hated being a mother, shame in that she believed no one would be there to lead her through the gates of heaven, shame that she deemed herself unworthy, that her life didn't matter, that she didn't matter.

Death is an event. Dying is a process. Over the nearly twenty-five years of caring for people, I have yet to meet someone who wasn't afraid of dying. It isn't in our nature to not be. Comfortingly, all humans seemingly traverse a common pathway of death. We will hold off on going into those details until later chapters, but here, it is important to know that dying does confront us with the reality of our lives—all the good, the bad, and the ugly. Some of the fear of dying stems from the knowing that we must "pay the piper," "face the music," "reap what we've sown." To this end, deathbed confessions are riddled with stories of shame.

Rooted in the experiences of harm—given and received—stories of shame are held on to and serve as the primary yet often hidden plot lines in the narrative of people's lives. Wishing to no longer carry the weight of such a burden, they find the courage to create space for these sufferings, transmuting their pain of separation and disconnection. Ironically, these patients frequently profess to anyone who will hear: "Don't wait! Don't wait till death visits your door. Make the effort *now* to repair and reconnect to what matters most!"

Jo was no exception. She shared all of it. Pouring out of her, shame was joined by forgiveness, relief, humor, joy, awe, and love. In those last days, Jo had finally opened to her full existence, and with it, she knew where she belonged.

But how? How does one purposely engage with the suffering of shame, pausing to open to our darkest parts while securely attaching to others and the world around so we may break through to the satisfaction of belonging?

CONNECTION: DO I MATTER?

Our major finding is that your history of relational health—your connectedness to family, community, and culture—is more predictive of your mental health than your history of adversity. Connectedness has the power to counterbalance adversity.

— OPRAH WINFREY AND DR. BRUCE PERRY,
WHAT HAPPENED TO YOU?

Though it may feel a bit abrupt and cold, let's start by looking at shame through the lens of neuroscience. Shame and the physiologic foundation of our need for connection rest in a rule of threes: a brain divided into three parts, three essential networks, and three domains of connection. Earlier, we examined the tripartite brain and its sequential processing. This processing is further refined by an additional trio of intertwined core networks—regulatory (stress), reward, and relational—mirroring the three fundamental domains of connection—those to the external world, to ourselves, and with others.[1]

Human

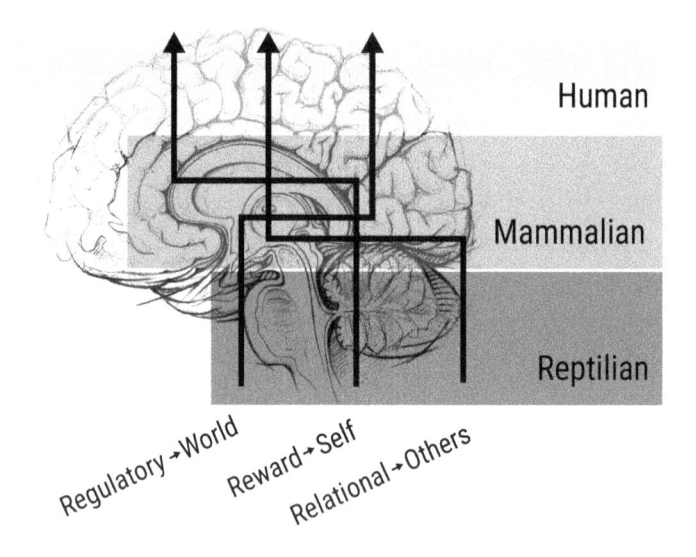

Mammalian

Reptilian

Regulatory→World   Reward→Self   Relational→Others

At the most primitive level, we are primarily connected to the world through the doors of our five senses. Taking in, relating to, and creating our experience of the world begins with sights, sounds, smells, tastes, and touches. As external events and internal information rise through sequential processing, the brain uses the core networks to filter exponential amounts of information, learn what is salient, and create functional memories in an effort to predict meaning, automate reactions, and maintain homeostasis. The basic elements of homeostasis include maintaining a steady state, managing dynamic change, fostering cooperation, and enforcing governance. Simply, a set of physiologic rules—demanding cooperation across the various organ systems to respond to the changing dynamics of context and circumstance with a primary goal of maintaining an optimal state of stability—govern the body.[2]

Our adaptive capacities of arousal and dissociation kick in with these sensory inputs, prompting reactions along the regulatory, stress response pathway we discussed previously. Everything from daydreaming and creativity to terror and catatonia depend on how we are connected to the world. Implicitly, disconnection occurs in the deprivation or exploitation of resources and the consequential threat of uncertainty. As we have already seen, when we don't have the basic necessities of life met, the suffering of fear pervades our experience. Explicitly, poverty and overconsumption both signal our disconnection from the world and along with it the often-added hidden feeling of shame. Consequently, many of us have lost our homeostatic relationship with the environment.

The reward network builds on the regulatory mechanisms to reinforce the binary system of moving toward pleasure and away from pain. Our reward system, while navigating the interface between the sensory input and our homeostatic stability, serves to introduce us to our sense of self—what we like and what we don't. Each day, our homeostatic stability depends on a certain amount of reward to accumulate. Guided by salience, our nervous system is attuned to seeking pleasure in novelty and intensity. Food—especially in a combination of sweet, salt, and fat—provides a significant dose of reward, as do other substances like alcohol and drugs.

Certain substances, like cocaine and heroin, can even directly activate the reward system. Interestingly, though, we can get confused between seeking pleasure for pleasure's sake or seeking pleasure to relieve distress. The relief of distress is significantly more rewarding to the nervous system, given our negativity bias, and is the reason we reach out to these material goods for soothing and why we are at risk for addiction. All pleasure has a touch of sourness, and all pain a touch of sweetness.[3]

Finally, the relational system of emotions and feelings attempts to broaden our experience, particularly in the reinforcement of our connection to others. As calls to action, emotions harness our attention and point us toward salient stimuli with emotive direction. Based on our current state of homeostasis and reward deficit, emotions, if unchecked, are often the nidus for impulsive behavior. Emotions are also contagious, and when you have two or more nervous systems neurobiologically intertwined, things can get a little messy. Does the experience of "hangry" ring a bell? Or how about the tense holiday dinner with your parents and siblings?

Together these networks cross-function to satisfy our need for connection, as "[a] person's capacity to connect, to be regulating and regulated, to reward and be rewarded, is the glue that keeps families and communities together."[4] The reward system responds to relational experiences and, pound for pound, we receive much more sustainable reward from our relationships as compared to the use of material goods and substances. Additionally, the relational aspect of our regulatory system is primarily developed through the attunement and attachment of those closest to us. Our families of origin are the sources for our first experiences of safety and trust, and our families of choice are from whom we continue to draw and sustain this powerful pool of regulatory reward. In essence, we are neurobiologically connected to the people closest to us, as our survival and flourishing depend on it.[5]

Sequential processing and the regulatory, reward, and relational networks collaborate to bolster the prediction function of the brain. If the rudimentary brain is built on a survival bias, the mammalian brain is built on a negativity bias.[6] Foundationally, it seems we are a "glass is half empty" kind of species. Constantly looking for the bad in the room, this negativity bias drives us to perpetually scan, prepare, and eliminate any and all threats to our homeostatic ideal. In our world of contrasting dualities, the environment is inherently chaotic and unpredictable. Illuminated by the powers of pleasure and pain, our prediction function primarily navigates the contrast between the dualities of threat and safety. As open systems, we are wired to instinctively and impulsively react to this tension with binary modes of if/then, yes/no, good/bad, either/or—moving toward pleasure, away from pain.

Unfortunately, in social circumstances, the dynamics of our survival and negativity biases can have far-reaching consequences. Though highly efficient, the prediction-to-reaction function of the brain can be a source of significant suffering, particularly as it relates to the need for connection.

When we sustain an experience that challenges our basic need for connection, it typically involves some sort of "injury, misunderstanding, invalidation, exclusion, or humiliation" and can come from being harmed or from being the one to cause the harm.[7] Depending on context, this challenge registers a sense of insecurity. In its most intense form, this insecurity arises as shame.

Unwanted, uncontrollable, and unbearable, the suffering of shame is the consequential distress of a real or perceived disconnection from the world, others, and ourselves, and as researcher and storyteller Dr. Brené Brown achingly states, shame leaves us believing that we are flawed and unworthy.[8] If fear is about uncertainty, then shame is about vulnerability and insecurity.

"For all social animals…identity is the passcard to inclusion, and inclusion is the key to survival."[9] Race, ethnicity, gender, sexuality—our genetic identity—gets shaped by circumstance—nationality, religion, socioeconomic status, education. When we believe our "tribe" perceives us as "bad," we suffer. To add further insult to injury, reinforced by the stories, symbols, and rituals found within our communal structures of culture and society, this dichotomous split often infects us with what I lovingly call the *horrible case of the shoulds*. You should be this, should do that, you should, should, should. You are too much, you should be less. You are not enough, you should be more. "The 'shoulds' are the basis of our 'bargain with fate'; if we obey them, we believe we can magically control external realities, though in reality they lead to deep unhappiness…"[10]

Under these circumstances, individuals often rebel, conform, or surrender to the "limiting notions of potential that are dictated by others… We become…alienated…focused on a very narrow slice of who we are…looking outward for validation… We don't develop the incredible strengths that already lie within."[11] Rebelling, we commit acts of violence, toward others and toward self. Conforming, we see perfectionism, an active avoidance mechanism against experiencing shame where we live the mantra "please, perform, perfect."[12] Described "perfectly" by Brené Brown, "perfection is a self-destructive and addictive belief system that fuels this primary thought: If I look perfect, live perfectly, work perfectly, and do everything perfectly, I can avoid or minimize the painful feelings of shame, judgment, and blame."[13]

With my Catholic upbringing, for me, this type of shame rings with a tone of redemptive suffering, and I have seen it painfully run people in circles of "if I only do/am _____, then I will be loved." Carrying things one step further, rebelling and compliance can also end in a type of surrendering termed *learned helplessness*. A passive mind state, learned helplessness is based on a belief that no action will change circumstance. People experiencing learned helplessness live life "paralyzed," waiting for the next event to come along and determine their fate.[14]

Whether rebelling, conforming, or surrendering, our primitive social connection is conditional, leaving many of us insufficiently prepared to move from childhood into and through adulthood. Unmoored, listless, and lonely, we experience a compromised independence and may consequently suffer additional exposure to intense and/or chronically harmful circumstances. Our prediction-to-reaction model adapts to the unwanted, uncontrollable, unbearable suffering of those circumstances. While adaptive under the harmful conditions, this self-preserving model may become "stuck" and maladaptive as life evolves. This stuckness triggers the auto-perpetuating cycle of suffering the suffering of shame.

Nowhere else do I see this more than in the university students I teach each semester. First-year students, of whom many have never been away from home for more than a handful of days, find themselves thrown into a brand-new environment with little to no resources for connection. Insidious, shame masquerades as anxiety and restlessness, depression, and despair, or sometimes a waxing and waning of both. Easy to spot, as at the extremes, one side is curled over in their hoodies attempting to make themselves so small as to be invisible while the other is consuming everything they can get their hands on—food, sex, substances, social media, gaming, and more. Violence, sadly, rears its head across all collegiate communal spaces. These maladaptive behaviors actually draw them further and further into disconnection. It is like they are all walking around in circles with neon signs alternately blinking *Unseen, Lonely, Shamed*, yet blind to the others similarly plagued.

Like fear, shame also has pre-incident indicators. Shame has many nuanced presentations, but in my work, it repeatedly shows up with two painfully significant warning signs: loneliness and remorse.

Loneliness, the absence of meaningful social interaction, appears to be at epidemic levels. In May 2023, the US Surgeon General, Dr. Vivek Murthy, published an advisory "raising alarm bells" on the broad-reaching impacts of loneliness in the US.[15] Prior to taking office, Murthy also penned a book entitled, *Together: The Healing Power of Human Connection in a Sometimes Lonely World.* In it, he discusses the three types of crucial relationships needed in a human life: intimate, friend, and community.[16] He also shares the data that loneliness poses a significant threat to our mortality. On par with that of smoking, loneliness increases the risk of premature death by 25 percent.[17] Loneliness is not about the quantity of people you know; it is about the quality of social connection across one's key relationships. You can be in a crowd of people and feel lonely or be alone and feel perfectly content. Being alone does not equal being lonely.

Interestingly, loneliness has a substantial neurobiological footprint. Groundbreaking work in social neuroscience demonstrates how loneliness calls us "to act and repair what is lacking. In other words, loneliness motivates us to repair connections and strengthen social ties, which ensures the survival of our genes and contributes to our health and well-being."[18] However, if the loneliness is unaddressed and the need for connection goes unsatisfied, the stress response system takes over and moves us into a state of self-preservation and social hypervigilance as the prepotency of the need for safety trumps our need for connection.

Loneliness, "not only increases the explicit desire to connect or reconnect with others, but it also produces an implicit hypervigilance for social threats… This evolutionary theory of loneliness suggests that feeling socially isolated or on the social perimeter leads to increased surveillance of the social world and an unwitting focus on self-preservation."[19] Paradoxically, this self-preservation appears to perpetuate the cycle of disconnection and loneliness, spiraling further and further into the suffering of shame.

Remorse, shame's other common face, is often confused with regret. Experientially, I have come to see remorse in the hearts of those who have caused harm to themselves or others and wish the injury to have never happened. Regret, as we'll talk about in the suffering of isolation, is more about what we haven't done in our lives. Regardless, both emotions are powerful motivators from which to learn, repair, and forgive. In remorse, however, this harm is deeply emotional, especially when we've harmed ourselves. Causing a direct disconnection, harm and its remorse can either move us to repair the injury we have caused, or it can drop us into a state of deep loneliness propagated by negative emotional rumination, further worsening the disconnection. And with it, shame often ensues.

Loneliness and remorse lurk in the hallways of America's hospitals. During any given day on rounds, it is not uncommon to care for a patient living with a chronic disease like heart failure or emphysema who comes and goes from the hospital, as if it was a close family member's home. Well-known to the staff, these "frequent flyers," when given the opportunity, share stories of the deep loneliness and remorse caused by their illness. Tethered to their oxygen tanks and relegated to their recliners, patients live from hospital episode to hospital episode with little to no human contact in between.

I cared for one woman who said the only time she received any sort of human touch was when she came to the hospital, and she admitted, there had been several times she called 911 to come to the hospital just so she could be seen, touched, to "feel felt."[20] Over the years of her progressive disease, she had divorced her husband and purposefully alienated herself from her children and siblings. During her final and terminal hospitalization, she not only expressed her deep despair of loneliness, but she confessed a profound remorse for the emotional harm she intentionally brought to those she espoused to hold most dear, including herself. Though acts of reparation somewhat eased the suffering in those last days, the toll of her unattended shame remained with her until her last breath.

Shame is exquisitely painful both physically and mentally and, like fear, can strip us of perspective, throwing us into a storm of stress and shoulds. Shame's physical markers have been displayed in every movie about adolescence: time slows, heart sounds bound in our ears, breath hitches and spurts, heat crawls its way up our neck painting our cheeks aflame, eyes avert, head tips and twists away from the assaulting view. Often the subsequent movie scene finds the harmed character sequestered, alone, licking the social wounds of shame.

This intensity reflects the importance of connection to our lives. As a signal that the second most basic need is compromised, shame also inherently includes an element of fear. The first basic need for safety is prepotent to the need for connection, and as noted previously, each need and its spectrum of suffering and satisfaction is subsumed and carried to the next progressive need as it emerges to be experienced.

Brené Brown states that "shame is the fear of disconnection," reflecting the contribution of prepotent needs being partially met and unmet in any given circumstance.[21] When I care for people who are working to understand their basic needs and their suffering and satisfaction, to parse out and assess the need for connection and get to the heart of the social suffering of shame, I offer the inquiry of: *Do I matter?*

Mattering, as defined by psychologist and personality expert Dr. Gordon Flett, is "the personal sense of feeling significant and valued." This definition goes on to state that mattering is a "vital…psychological resource that is central to the human condition; indeed, the individual person who lives…devoid of a sense of mattering…will lack the basic sense of personal significance, human connectedness, and social acceptance required to thrive and flourish." Mattering is a "vital, universal, and powerful" aspect of our development and, when compromised, reflects the disconnect and risk of shame.[22]

When we ask, "Do I matter?" it sharply explores where, how, and to what extent we are disconnected from the world, others, and ourselves. When the suffering of shame appears, it is, simply and powerfully, a call to attend to our deep unmet need for connection.

INVOKING THE PAUSE

The more lonely and separate we feel, the more we turn to desires to compensate. We go through our day yanked by the chain of one desire after another until we finally lose touch with who we really are. Though the world may reward us for our drivenness, internally we are diminished.

— JACK KORNFIELD, *THE WISE HEART*

Desire, the wanting of wanting things to be different, directly reflects our suffering an unmet need for connection. But desire can be blinding in its effort to help us relieve our distress. Indulged or suppressed, the impulse of desire brings suffering itself, as it shoots us like a pinball, slung around aimlessly by the levers of pain and pleasure, threat and safety. We must acknowledge the power of negativity and security biases in order to open to the vulnerability of mattering to relieve our suffering of shame. Turning to Jack Kornfield, psychologist and beloved meditation teacher, to better articulate our mechanisms for managing desire and the pain of disconnection: "Aversion and hatred arise from a misguided search for security, from the mistaken belief that hatred can make us safer. And at the root of delusion itself is the illusion of a separate, limited sense of self."[23] True connection is not driven by the relief of desire (wanting, ambition, addiction) or hate (blame, aggression) or delusion (denial) but rather recognizing and learning to lean into the pain disconnection brings to our lives.

When we don't let go and hang on to these intensely negative emotions and feelings, desire and the spectrum of survival reactivity run amuck. We lose connection to ourselves and with it our senses and emotions drop into regulatory survival mode. Unethical, aggressive, and/or violent behavior typically involves shame fueled by fear and the arousal emotion of rage. Returning to Gavin de Becker and *The Gift of Fear*, "violence is a process that evolves over time; it is not a condition or a state." He continues, "Anger is very 'seductive'... [and when fueled by]...righteous indignation to being ignored, rejected, and erased...can be the engine for behavior that [someone] may have never considered before."[24]

Additionally, what happens if the violence is turned inward? In such pain, people collapse in anguish as a result of their shame, often turning to episodic overconsumption to dissociate and dull the intensity of disconnection. Used as self-soothing distraction, food, sex, substances, and even self-harm fill the hole shame carves into our bellies. Doomscrolling on social media, excessive gaming, and risky gambling also push the brain's reward system to seek more and more, explicitly demonstrating that shame is a fuel for the cycle of self-destructive behavior.

Expressions of self-harm have exploded over the last twenty years. Commenting on the relationship between the growth of the internet in our lives and violence, Gavin de Becker poignantly reflects: "the media age did bring a type of mass hypnosis into American life...when media consumption replaces the rest of life, it affects all of us to some degree, and some of us to a great degree... manipulating emotion and behavior toward institutional idolatry."[25]

The quantity and quality of violent, pornographic, self-absorbed virtual content has invaded our homes and our kids' lives. Dr.

Jonathan Haidt, social psychologist and author, explores the consequences of this invasion in his book entitled, *The Anxious Generation: How the Great Rewiring of Childhood Is Causing an Epidemic of Mental Illness*. In the chapter, "Tidal Wave: The Surge of Suffering," Haidt marches through the horrifying statistics. From 2010–2015, in what Haidt calls "the great rewiring," there appears to have been an inflection point where:

- Teenage depression and anxiety, termed *internalizing disorders* in psychiatry, steeply rose in a hockey-stick-like fashion. When compared between 2010–2020, teenage depression became two and a half times more prevalent.
- Emergency room visits for nonfatal self-injury in adolescent girls jumped an alarming 188 percent.
- Young adolescent (ten to fourteen years old) deaths by suicide rose 91 percent in boys and 167 percent in girls.[26]

In suffering, there are no quick fixes; rather it's more about learning to see into the uncertainty rather than be awash with the calls of unmet needs. It's about being comfortable with the uncomfortable. Continuing further with the work of Brené Brown, she lovingly states, "If we want to live and love with our whole hearts, and if we want to engage with the world from a place of worthiness, we have to talk about the things that get in the way—especially, shame, fear, and vulnerability."[27]

Recognizing shame is a deep, tender experience, what I am suggesting is meant to be a starting point, a place to just begin, to start now before the crisis occurs. Bearing in mind the external events and internal information that gave rise to the suffering of shame may need the security of a therapist or other qualified professional in order to be safely felt and processed.

Building upon practicing prediction and stabilizing attention, the satisfaction of our need for connection begins with learning to invoke a pause when any sense of disconnection, insecurity, vulnerability, or shame rises to the surface. While it seems oversimplified, I believe this pause is a true hallmark of human maturity, as it demonstrates profound responsibility and the recognition that we have an unmet basic need and may require help. The pause allows us to remain in the moment while giving the nervous system time to move out of the reactivity of instinct and impulse into more relational and purposeful responsiveness of intent and inspiration.

While many techniques are used to develop the pause, my favorite and the one I teach to students is a combination of two well-known mindfulness activities:

HALT, RAIN it in!

HALT, adapted from neuroscientist Dr. Jill Bolte Taylor calls to recognize the basic needs. When you experience a wave of distressing sensation/emotion/feeling/thought, HALT asks you to take a big deep breath, and inquire *Am I*:

H—Hungry?

A—Angry, Anxious, Apathetic?

L—Lonely?

T—Tired?[28]

Then RAIN it in! RAIN is a well-known Buddhist practice that moves us into observing our experiences. From psychiatrist and mindfulness researcher Dr. Jud Brewer:

R—Recognize and relax into what is arising

A—Allow it to be there

I—Investigate sensations, feelings, emotions, moods, images, thoughts

N—Nurture and note what you need[29]

The next time you find yourself experiencing an intense feeling or emotion, try to invoke the pause before reacting. It is a shockingly hard but very powerful way to remain connected to yourself and avoid harming others. As the essential first step to self-directed human development, the pause reclaims our attention from the lower brain centers and offers the time for our human brain to weigh in.

To expand a bit more on feelings, emotion, and moods, I'll refer to the work of Dr. Paul Ekman, one of the most influential psychologists of our time. In addition to being named one of *Time Magazine*'s one hundred most influential people, he significantly contributed to the science and development behind the Disney/Pixar *Inside Out* franchise. Ekman defines emotion as:

> "a process, a particular kind of automatic appraisal influenced by our evolutionary and personal past, in

which we sense that something important to our welfare is occurring, and a set of psychological changes and emotional behaviors begins to deal with the situation."[30]

Moods primarily differ from emotions in terms of duration and the use of the three core circuits. Per Ekman, "when we speak of an emotion lasting for an extended amount of time (hours), it's more likely that we are summating recurrent emotional episodes within that timeframe and not actually experiencing a constant and consistent emotion. Moods, however, can last for hours, sometimes even days, and can be difficult to shake."[31] In the psychological literature, "mood is a pervasive and sustained emotion that colors the perception of the world." In layman's terms, "*mood* refers to a more pervasive and sustained…'climate,' [verses] the emotional 'weather.'"[32] And feeling? It is the cognitively integrated experience of sustained mood and arising emotion in any given moment.[33]

Ekman's work also proposes the concept of the seven universal emotions—fear, anger, sadness, surprise, disgust, contempt, and enjoyment—and that they "are innate and shared by everyone, and that they are accompanied across cultures by universal facial expressions."[34] Together with the more self-conscious emotions—embarrassment and humiliation, jealousy and envy, sympathy and empathy, pride and hubris, regret and remorse—these seven universal emotions begin to display themselves in our early childhood, motivating us to develop from dependence to independence.

These emotions are primarily oriented to the outside world and our relationships with others, and through our relationship with others we begin the process of understanding our mattering in the world. Guilt is also one of these key self-conscious emotions and can help us to understand how our behavior impacts others. The literature simply frames guilt as the emotion of feeling "I did something bad." However, when guilt merges with disgust, we see these relational emotions make a combined U-turn to render shame, the emotion and feeling of "I am bad." Where guilt is about behavior and can be motivational, shame is about self-insecurity and is corrosive, as shame can be described as self-disgust.[35]

Invoking the pause creates space for the naming and allowing of big emotions and tensions to be fully felt and processed, to be comfortable with the uncomfortable. Often, it seems that the residue of unprocessed experiences mucking up the sequential processing system leads to suffering in the first place. As Bolte Taylor suggests, "Because we are feeling creatures who have the capacity to think, instead of running our emotional circuitry on automatic [reactivity], we have the power to choose to push the pause button, wait for ninety seconds while the physiology of our emotions flushes out of our body, and then choose the life we want to live."[36] In allowing the fullness of our experience, the good and the bad, we can first belong to ourselves.

Once paused and emotions are safely and fully allowed, we can purposefully cultivate our environment of sights, sounds, smells, tastes, and touch to better align with and connect to the world at large. Our body is equipped with profound therapeutic capability. Breathwork, drumming, music, and movement are literally right at our fingertips and readily accessible to support us in practicing the pause to process. Rhythm regulates us, allowing us to relate.[37]

The environment has become supersaturated and overstimulating. Artificial light and processed food have moved us further and further away from what Native American author Robin Wall Kimmerer calls our "original instructions." In her book, *Braiding Sweetgrass,* Kimmerer beautifully relays the deep connection we must cultivate with nature so that we may "'use [our] gifts and dreams for good' and through...actions of reciprocity...living... to take care of the land as if our lives, both material and spiritual, depended on it."[38] Our connection to the world, particularly through the natural and purposeful use of our sensory and reward systems, sets the foundation for our satisfaction of belonging.

Only with the quieting of our stress response and reward systems can we begin to relate to others. Meeting our shame as a call to connect empowers us to express our needs and trust that they will be met. As adults, we must do this for ourselves so we can create the deep connection essential to the health of the children in our lives. Remembering that we were once children too, we honor the foundational connections evolution demands we have with others—be attuned, receive affection, and allow for us to matter, to fully feel felt, and to know that we belong.

ATTACHMENT

What is believed to be essential for mental health is that the infant and young child should experience a warm intimate and continuous relationship with his caregiver in which both find satisfaction and enjoyment.

— DR. JOHN BOWLBY, *ATTACHMENT AND LOSS*

As children, we are dependent upon others to regulate our environment and help us remain secure. This state of dependency is the longest of any other known species.[39] Consequently, humans are evolutionarily social creatures, and our familial, societal, and ecological circumstances diametrically support and challenge us. Overcoming this tension is one of our most difficult developmental tasks, as we are products of our experiences of attachment with, attunement from, and trust in others and the world at large.

John T. Cacioppo, cofounder of the field of social neuroscience and expert in loneliness, best shared his insights to attachment in his still relevant 2013 TEDx:

> "…social species, by definition, create merging structures that extend beyond an organism, structures that range from couples and families to schools and nations and cultures. These structures evolved hand-in-hand with neural, hormonal, and genetic mechanisms to support them because the consequent social behavior helps these organisms survive, reproduce, and leave a genetic legacy. To grow into an adulthood for a social species, including humans, is not to become autonomous and solitary, it's to become the one on whom others can depend. Whether we know it or not, our brain and biology have been shaped to favor this outcome."[40]

Like survival, we are also hardwired for connection.

In the 1950–60s, Drs. John Bowlby and Mary Ainsworth famously described what is known as Attachment

Theory. Their research laid the foundation for the current understandings of our need for connection. In parallel with our fear response system, our attachment system develops as a necessary mechanism for survival. As small children, trouble always finds us, and when it does, we seek care to help us deal with the overwhelming experiences of fear, all its faces, and the threat behind it. Our *attachment style*, which is how we give and receive care, is initially shaped by the responsiveness of our primary childhood caregivers, as they lend us their adult senses of self to foster the scaffolding of what will be our future selves and how we will relate to the world and others.[41]

Based on our experiences of receiving comfort in times of stress, attachment styles develop along a spectrum of secure to insecure, shaped by the two main coping strategies—avoidance and anxiety. Based on this spectrum, adults manifest four primary attachment styles:

1. Secure (Low avoidance, low anxiety)
2. Preoccupied (Low avoidance, high anxiety)
3. Fearful-avoidant (High avoidance, high anxiety)
4. Dismissing-avoidant (High avoidance, low anxiety)

As summarized by humanistic psychologist and Maslow expert Dr. Scott Barry Kaufman, "The anxious-attachment dimension reflects a concern about being rejected and abandoned and is the product of beliefs about whether others will be there for you in times of need. The avoidant-attachment dimension has less to do with a sense of safety and more to do with how you regulate your emotions in response to stress—whether you use others as a secure base or pull away and withdraw from them."[42] In terms of secure attachment, if safety is about having the shelter of physical house, connection is about having the belonging of a home.

Unfortunately, many parents are underresourced to provide a secure base from which children can safely come and go to explore and learn about the world. Parenting is a communal act, as summarized by a recent work updating the theory:

> "Bowlby stresses the view that the healthy development of adults from infancy onward—and the avoidance of the development of psychopathology—lies not only in the hands of parents but also in the hands of the culture and the availability of support for parents."[43]

To this end, Gavin de Becker, in *The Gift of Fear,* gives a chilling account of his own violent childhood and the importance of children having multiple early attachment figures: "terribly unhealthy families damage children in many ways, but one of the saddest is the destruction of the child's belief that he has purpose and value. Without that belief, it is difficult to succeed, difficult to take risks…they are not up to the task, [but] if a child has some effective human contact at particularly significant periods, some recognition of his worth and value, some 'witness' to his experience, this can make an extraordinary difference. No ceremony attaches to the moment that a child sees his own worth reflected in the eyes of an encouraging adult."[44]

As a kid, I was enveloped by a Celtic ethos heavily influenced by Roman Catholicism. The clan mentality was to hoard food, pass judgment, and wield anger as a weapon as if we still were living in an ancient war. Born to teenage parents yet surrounded by a large family of great-grandparents, grandparents, aunts, and uncles, I was fortunate enough to have a web of caregivers ensuring my basic needs were being met and protecting me from the cruel side of our family way. Additionally, my kindergarten teacher was a godsend in those early years of my life. However, when, at the age of nine, my parents moved us cross-country from a sprawling metropolis to a quaint, very rural town that was thousands of miles away, the safety net of our extended family vanished and the full breadth of our family's insecurity showed itself.

Often left to my own defenses to care for myself and for my younger siblings, I picked up the clan's sword and along with it loads of anger that was managed with loads of food. Needless to say, I entered the world of adulthood with a scarcity, sword-out mentality that did not set me up well for adult friend and intimate relationships. Through counseling and the development of key relationships, I found my way through the hungry and angry shame of my childhood. The integration of my past by the active rewiring of my neural networks toward more connection allowed me to be wholly with others, identify and exercise life by my values, and find joy in the world.

Reflecting our need for safety and need for connection, we need to fully develop two primary functions of caregiving. The first form of caregiving is empathetic and meant to offer protection, soothing, and comfort when seeing distress. The second form of caregiving, building on the first, functions to share in the personal interest of the seeker and be competent in helping the seeker to make sense of the world and plan for a safe future. Both of these caregiving elements are essential to securely attached relationships whether they are parental, peer, or partner. They are also both foundational to a secure relationship with ourselves.[45]

Going back to "naming the water," I share these insights not to point blame but to give air to things that may be hidden in the plain sight of your connections to self, others, and the world. As studies have shown, "there is only little continuity between early childhood…and adult attachment patterns…our current attachment patterns are influenced by our entire history of relationships and social interactions."[46] Returning to Dr. Murthy's triad of essential relationships—intimate, friends and family, and community connections, we can use the attachment science to look at the health of these relationships and how we attach, how we connect.[47] Additionally, we can also see where we might be attached to things—food, drugs, virtual reality, money, possessions—as substitutes for real connection. Finally, we can reflect on how secure we are in the relationship to our developing sense of self.

BELONGING

Fromm writes, "Infantile love follows the principle: 'I love because I am loved.' Mature love follows the principle 'I am loved because I love.' Immature love says, 'I love you because I need you.' Mature love says, 'I need you because I love you.'"
—SCOTT BARRY KAUFMAN, *TRANSCEND*

When our need for connection is met, we know we matter as well as where and with whom we belong. Unmet, our need for connection calls out in the most raw and painful experiences of being human; it calls out to the social and redemptive suffering of shame. Impulsively, we react with our emotions, seeking out material objects and experiences to soothe the pain of loneliness and remorse. When we feel shame, we believe we are "flawed and therefore unworthy," and our ability to develop a worthwhile sense of self becomes untenable.

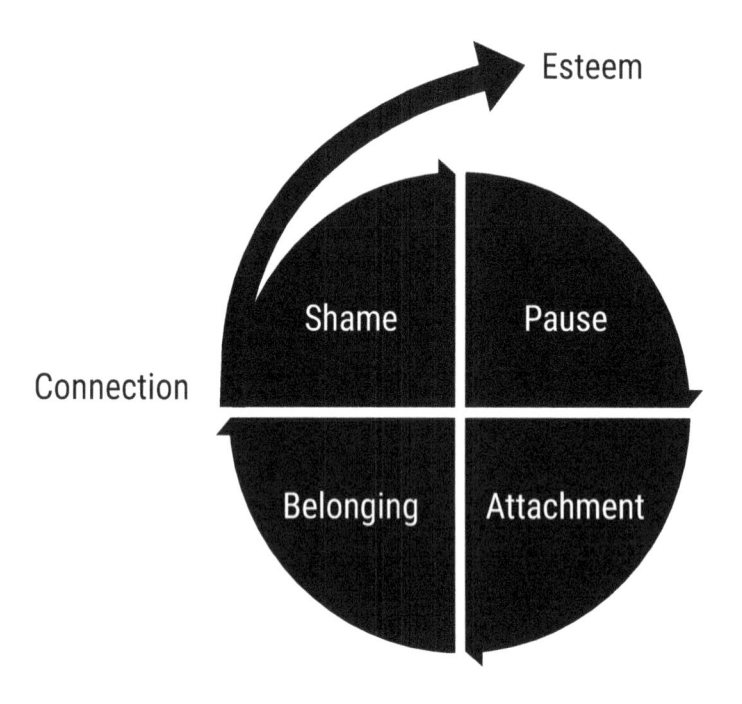

Esteem

Connection

Shame | Pause

Belonging | Attachment

If shame is the suffering of the unmet need for connection, ten belonging is its satisfaction. When we experience "being seen, understood, and accepted by an attuned, empathetic other... a sense of genuine self-acceptance, a feeling that we are profoundly okay. We feel safe enough, strong enough, sure enough to venture courageously into the world and develop the competencies we need to deal with life's challenges."[48] Brené Brown beautifully describes the satisfaction of connection as:

> "The energy that exists between people when they feel seen, heard, and valued; when they can give and receive without judgment; and when they derive sustenance and strength from the relationship."[49]

Brown goes on to say, "Knowing and applying the language of human experience and emotion is key to [supporting] meaningful connection."[50] Clearly providing the language of connection and its experiential spectrum of shame and belonging helps us take the first step on the arduous road of effectively satisfying one of our most basic needs.

Over and over, I sit at bedsides where the events of an illness or impending death have revealed a chronically unmet need for connection, the suffering of shame, and the desperate will to reach toward the satisfaction of belonging. Upon sharing this sentiment, a colleague who is a hospice nurse reminded me of a quote by Norm Cousins, a journalist who experienced serious illness, "Death is not the ultimate tragedy of life. The ultimate tragedy is depersonalization—dying in an alien and sterile area, separated from the spiritual nourishment that comes from being able to reach out to a loving hand, separated from the desire to experience the things that make life worth living, separated from hope."[51]

Using the power of suffering, patients and families welcome each and every member to authentically "be" who they are. Brené Brown continues with a reminder that it takes vulnerability, integrity, and courage to "learn how to be present with people without sacrificing who we are" and to share our shame stories, especially as we seek to repair and heal broken connections.[52]

Like shame, belonging can feel like some outside force that is bestowed upon us. Yet, what I have seen is that belonging, like the other satisfactions, is always quietly present and must be revealed through repeated acts of pausing and securely attaching. Knowing we have choices in how we belong seems to recover some of the insecurity and unpredictability we so often feel in life. In these moments at the bedside, I have come to appreciate and understand that connection happens through actively revealing the belonging of our lives. Invoking the pause and securely attaching, we transform the suffering of shame into the recognition that *I do matter.*

Our health and well-being are deeply biologically rooted in *where* we live, and with *whom* we live on a day-to-day basis. Most importantly, however, the key to meeting our need for connection resides in *how* we live and *what* choices we make. We receive the most substantial reward experience from exercising our personal beliefs and values, the belonging to one's self.

Self-security is "openly and nonjudgmentally accepting [the] things that challenge our sense of self-worth." As first articulated in research conducted at University of Illinois Urbana-Champaign, self-security is essential to our understanding of others' evaluative perceptions, aptness to be emotionally vulnerable, and capacity to be realistic about what we can do without the need to "aggrandize" ourselves.[53] Self-security contributes to our attachment style and can greatly influence the quality of our relationships. It is also tied to shame-proneness. As we will see, self-security is the prepotent aspect of connection that underpins the need for self-esteem. Simply, self-security fosters our ability to be fully seen and as a consequence, "feel fully felt."[54]

In a closing comment, you may have noticed that I have pulled love out of the hierarchy. In Maslow's theory, love was paired with belonging as a satisfaction of the need for connection. Diverting from Maslovian tradition, I believe love is the container from which the hierarchy itself arises. Maslow spoke to the significant differences in the expressions of D-love, the form of deficiency love often paired with dependence and belonging, relative to the more spiritual B-love of interdependence, he described as the "love for the being of another person."[55]

This difference is idealized in the Fromm epigraph above. Evidenced by its many faces—familial, friendly and flirtatious, personal and passionate, companionable and communal—love is the universal presence on which all experience and, as a consequence, our needs exist. Love is the still background to the vacillating pandemonium of life's daily sufferings and satisfactions, even when we suffer in the disconnection of shame.

And, when one speaks of love, one must also speak of loss. Grief, love left unexpressed, is one of the most raw, complicated emotions we experience as humans, and depending on the state of a human's development and the threat to survival a loss may provoke, grief can manifest as any one or all of the sufferings.

Love and loss whisper in each of the needs.

Becoming Needs and the Sufferings of Self

What is necessary to change a person is to change his awareness of himself.

—ABRAHAM MASLOW

As already mentioned, we have neurobiological machinery that compels us toward survival. Fear, driven by rage and anguish, and its manifestations—such as hunger, thirst, fatigue, pain, and stress—all motivate us to attend to the physicality of our safety needs. Meanwhile, shame, in its forms of loneliness and remorse, motivates us to seek connections that expand and reinforce our secure attachments. With enough safety and connection, our sense of self materializes, prompting the developmental shift from dependence to independence, and we begin the journey toward becoming a free-standing, contributing member of our community.

If our basic needs—safety and connection—concern the body and our relationship to the external world, our becoming needs—esteem and exploration—pertain to the mind, its budding sense of self, and our relationship to our internal world. Before we delve into the depths of the mind, it's important to acknowledge that the mind and body are two sides of the same coin. This seems intellectually obvious to most people, me included. However, when I began to truly explore the experience of my own body-mind connection, I found (and have subsequently found in many patients) that I had lived the large majority of my life in my head, the perceived location of my mind, as I found it safer than my body.

As an infant, I underwent serial castings of my lower legs to support an undefined laxity in both ankles. Seemingly, the first eight months of my life were lived in a sea of pain, and in a form of self-preserving defense, my young mind learned a trick of living just outside its body. Because of this, I came to "feel" and understand my body from a completely observational view. Until my early thirties, I was totally oblivious to this sleight of hand my mind had played to deal with the pain of my body. Though I was not particularly fond of my body and saw it more as a nuisance of living, I actually prided myself on what I believed was a high level of interoceptive awareness and emotional intelligence. That is, until I underwent hypnosis training.

Pediatric palliative care providers often learn hypnosis to help young patients cope with the pains of serious illness. By teaching these children to harness the adaptability of their developing brains and minds, they can learn to live with their disease rather than be defined by it. Ironically, it seems my very young brain had precociously adapted to this concept.

One of the key teachings in hypnosis training is that all hypnosis is self-hypnosis, demanding the therapist first step into the role of the patient as a firsthand experience. So the practice, initially, felt inaccessible, as I was completely unaware of my already adapted mind state. My mentor, a wise and highly practiced pediatric palliative care attending, took me through a hypnotic process and asked my mind a simple question: "What does your body feel like *from the inside*?" and in a split second, I came to "know" myself for what seemed like the very first time.

In this watershed moment, I came to realize my own ignorance to the relationship between my mind and body and came to directly understand the obviousness of splitting the mind from the body is tantamount to splitting water from the ocean. As you can imagine, life after that experience was markedly different and, at times, quite challenging, yet it became much richer and much more authentic.

This profound shift in perspective unveiled a deep sense of agency that had previously been out of reach. By recognizing that the truths of both my body and my mind could be held simultaneously, I developed a profound curiosity. Aspired to understand, I came to appreciate how the sufferings of the self, ignorance and judgment, collectively call us to heal the body-mind split—one of the oldest wounds in the human psyche.

The wound is attributed to the seventeenth-century French philosopher René Descartes, who authored *A Discourse on the Method*, an ode to logic and reason that has stood the test of time. Brilliant and fiercely rational, Descartes greatly influenced the exploding worlds of seventeenth-century science and mathematics. In *Discourse*, he famously exclaimed, "I think, therefore I am," and the Cartesian body-mind split was born. The then-nascent practice of modern medicine consequently dedicated itself to the exploration of the body, split from the mind as the mind, at that time, was understood to be part of the spirit and was a holy subject to be handled solely by the church.[1]

We are still living the consequences of the split today—science split from spirituality, physical split from mental, material split from mystery. Just one look at the healthcare system and you see hospitals dedicated to treating the diseases of the body physically separated from those treating the diseases of the mind, and they are even regulated under different processes.

Excitingly, the combined efforts of integrative medical practices on the scientific side and the contemplative practices on the spiritual side have invigorated our commitment to healing this dastardly split, and we are now seeing exponential growth in medical uses of meditation and mindfulness in the treatment of physical disease. Additionally, the burgeoning crossover practices like *psychoneuroimmunology*, the field dedicated to healing the interrelatedness between the nervous system, immunologic, and endocrine functions and the psyche of the mind are bridging the previously impossible divide.[2]

In the seminars and retreats I have led, so much of the suffering addressed is consequential to healing individuals' body-mind splits. Like the brain, the mind is multilayered, and the need for esteem primarily emerges to foster the development of our sense of self, the base layer of the mind related to the experience of the body. Distinguished research professor and historian Lynn Hunt articulated it as: "Having a sense of self as the protagonist in the ongoing experiences of the body is crucial to consciousness, and ultimately to a sense of agency and identity. This sense of self emerges from the mind's interpretations of the body's interactions in the world."[3] Healing this wound of disembodiment through understanding and directly experiencing the self is the next essential step on the travels toward its actualization.

The concept of self and its neurological correlates are fodder for hot debate. The sense of self cannot be tangibly located anywhere in the brain or body, despite the fact many of us can attest to navigating the world from a subjective viewpoint often perceived to originate in the middle part of the head, just behind the eyes.

For millennia, experts in both science and spirituality have attempted to universally define the phenomenon of the self, yet despite being championed by much loved physician-philosopher William James, furthered by the findings of psychoanalysis done by Sigmond Freud and Carl Jung, and continued today in the probing field of neuropsychotherapy, our collective exploration of the sense of self still remains frustratingly inconclusive. Precious to us all, as it is the *I, me, mine* of existence, perhaps reimagining suffering may offer us further insight to this core component of our nature.

Beginning around the age of two with the toddler screams of "mine, mine, mine" and extending toward the follies of teenage angst, the sense of self adaptively develops, and despite being impermanent and ever-changing, it allows for an illusory psychological continuity that we refer to as "I." Many may know this "I" as the ego. Again, another issue of language arises, as our sufferings of ignorance and judgment are reflected in the chaos of self-referential language that includes use of words like I, ego, self (both lowercase and upper case), my, me, mine, body, mind, soul, spirit, etc. What do we really mean when we say the word "I"? As offered by psychiatrist Daniel Lieberman:

> "In English, the word ego has a negative connotation because it's typically associated with being conceited. But in Latin, it's neutral. It simply translates to the word *I*. Psychiatrists use the word ego as a technical term for the person *I* refers to, as in, 'I enjoyed that movie.' They use this technical term because the ego, the I, is not the only personality inside your head. There are many others, and although you may not be aware of them, they control your life in profound ways."[4]

In addition to attempting to clarify the language issue, Lieberman also introduces this idea that we are all walking around with multiple parts to our self, further complicating yet elucidating the causes of the sufferings of self. While this may take some of you by surprise and raise a significant amount of weariness or concern for others, the multiplicity concept of self has been hinted at throughout the history of psychological studies.

As exemplified by the work of the Italian psychiatrist Roberto Assagioli, a contemporary of Jung and Freud, the study of our multiple nature has captured the eye of many luminaries in the fields of psychology, theology, and philosophy. Assagioli, inspired by the work of William James and Jung, asserted that we naturally develop identity patterns called subpersonalities, and the actualization of the self is done through psychosynthesis, an integration of the subpersonalities. As consequences of the changing social roles we have across our lifetime, Assagioli suggests our subpersonalities are shaped by:

- What we believe ourselves to be
- What we would like to be
- How we believe others see us
- What we want to appear to be
- What we believe we can become[5]

Assagioli's psychosynthesis work and other similar models set the stage for the modern-day study of self as a system of parts. Led by psychotherapist Dr. Richard Schwartz, "parts" therapy, or what is scientifically known as Internal Family Systems (IFS), has developed a "new model of the mind" that undeniably recognizes and embraces its multiplicity. Building on the premises of sequential processing and psychosynthesis, Schwartz further refines the definition of self as "a collection of parts that…are protectors who are simply trying to keep us safe and are reacting to and containing other parts that carry emotions and memories from [the] past." Plainly, parts reflect the younger versions of ourselves who live within and influence our experiences and behavior in the everyday present yet operate from their perspective stuck in the unprocessed histories of our past.[6]

Schwartz continues, "...all of us are born with many sub-minds that are constantly interacting inside of us. This in general is what we call *thinking*, because the parts are talking to each other and to you constantly about the thing you have to do or debating the best course of action, and so on."[7] Returning to the writings of David Foster Wallace, the sufferings of the self, ignorance and judgment, are truly about "'learning how to 'think'...learning how to exercise some control over *how* and *what* you think. It means being conscious and aware enough to *choose* how you construct meaning from experience..."[8]

Marrying the work discussed earlier by Perry and Assagioli, IFS strives to identify and "unburden" parts, freeing them from the suffering of their protective roles to perform higher functions of mind.[9] Recognizing our suffering as the undeveloped parts of ourselves that have unmet basic and becoming needs reflects what Maslow suggested when he stated, "if therapy means a pressure toward breaking controls and inhibitions, then our new key words must be spontaneity, release, naturalness, self-acceptance, impulse awareness, gratification, self-choice. If our intrinsic impulses are understood to be admirable rather than detestable, we shall certainly wish to free them for their fullest expression rather than to bind them into straitjackets."[10]

The imperative nature of the self and its parts to protect and stabilize is reinforced by our basic needs of safety and connection. Depending on the environment, our child-like self is highly adapted to our dependence stage of development, but if it is defined to manage unmanageable stress and if we don't recognize and readapt accordingly, it restricts our growth as adults, thwarting our independence. In an effort to remain safe and connected, this childlike, multiple self lulls us into a hypnotic amalgamation of sensations, emotions, memories, thoughts, roles, and responsibilities shaped to protect the "me" of our existence.

Through the strength of these protective parts, the sense of self draws us into a false identification, and in this misidentification, we suffer ignorance and judgment. In suffering, the self faces the ultimate of choices: 1) it can cling to its parts and the ever-changing roles, desires, and trappings of the external world that give shape to it, or 2) it can let go and open into the unknown ineffability of a primally known greater existence, to the core essence of who or what we really are.

The sense of self is a necessary yet precarious faculty that us humans must learn to recognize, navigate, and refine. First expressed through our constitution, our unique body-mind complex, the sense of self is primarily shaped by our genetics, epigenetics, and early childhood experiences. Simply, our physical features and mental temperament give us the filter and consequential perspective from which we view the world.

We develop preferences and quirks and operate on habits and routines. Roles and accomplishments further shape and define the self, but the sufferings of ignorance and judgment call us to seek something beyond these impermanent structures. Our ability to recognize "self" is the uniquely human capacity that serves as the basis by which the "man who knows he knows" knows himself and is what differentiates his consciousness from other mammals. Allowed to mature, this "self-consciousness" comes to understand that we are not our parts—our bodies, our minds, emotions, sensations, images, feelings, or thoughts—yet in this recognition, the self is confronted with the staggering question of *if I am not that, then who am I?*

As best said by Carl Jung, "Until you make the unconscious conscious, it will direct your life, and you will call it fate." Jung believed that our parts come together to form the self.[11] Embracing the knowledge found in satisfying our esteem needs prepares us to explore its application to our own direct experience. We become familiar with the identity tied to the self and move from dependence to independence. As the nuances of the sense of self are appreciated, the becoming needs are satisfied, readying us to plumb the depths of our unconscious and engage with our inner parts. The prepotency of basic and becoming needs provides the crucial developmental power needed to meet our being needs, enabling a holistic transition from independence to interdependence.

The primary playground for heeding the calls of the sufferings of ignorance and judgment and healing the body-mind split is to personally understand and directly experience what we define as the "self." Gaining perspective and exercising agency engenders the satisfaction of knowledge in the self and opens us to lean into its multiplicity, its roles and capacities. Ignorance worked toward self-knowledge also affords us the willingness to grow and the courage to explore the world at large where we learn to exercise our capacity to hold paradox and invoke aspiration, transforming the suffering of judgment into the satisfaction of curiosity and readying us for interdependence.

Embracing this inherent self-knowledge and moving from the satisfaction of esteem needs to the pursuit of exploration represents a key turning point in our uniquely human development. This shift aligns with Maslow's concept of motivation transitioning from a focus on deficiency needs to one of growth.[12] Our becoming needs mark the transition where our evolutionary inheritance as reptiles and mammals evolves into our distinct evolutionary responsibility as humans.

Ignorance.

To each his suff'rings: all are men,
Condemn'd alike to groan,
The tender for another's pain;
Th'unfeeling for his own.
Yet ah! why should they know their fate?
Since sorrow never comes too late,
And happiness too swiftly flies.
Thought would destroy their paradise.
No more; where ignorance is bliss,
'Tis folly to be wise.

—THOMAS GRAY, ODE ON A DISTANT PROSPECT OF ETON COLLEGE

One of the most significant changes we must endure as humans involves moving from dependence to independence. Typically, this transition parallels the path of physical development from infancy, through childhood, to adolescence, and finally young adulthood. Young adulthood, chronologically those who are eighteen to forty years of age (yes, forty!), marks a significant point of transition in our development where we have gained the bio-psycho-social capacities to realize the potentialities of healthy independence. Ideally, this growth marches in parallel to the satisfaction of our basic needs, allowing for the emergence of the need for esteem and empowering a young person to "see" themselves and their role in the world at large. Requisite to the need for exploration and the higher being needs, the satisfaction of esteem is pivotal to actualization. As Maslow could arguably be summarized by saying, the point of creating the self is a means to transcend it.[1]

The sense of self brings psychological consistency to our lives, making living with impermanence tolerable, yet we are still subject to the ever-present cycle of change. The unending loop of creation, transformation, and dissolution is the most challenging dynamic for homeostasis, as it often leaves us breathless, clinging to an "I" that is in continuous evolution. In resisting change, there is the extraordinary, unnecessary suffering of ignorance. Overidentified with the illusory "I," those who suffer ignorance remain trapped in a developmental limbo.

A poorly defined or deployed sense of self can appear as a locked-in experience of emotional immaturity that leads to what humanistic psychologist Scott Barry Kaufman calls *psychological entropy*. He states, "all biological organisms— including humans—survive insofar as they are able to effectively manage internal entropy."[2] This entropy, a term used in systems thinking, is a state of disorder represented by the movement away from a state of stable coherence (i.e. homeostasis) toward uncertainty, which leads to disruption and distress of the system (i.e. suffering). Kaufman, quoting

Maslow, goes on to say that the reduction of internal entropy "is critical not only to health and wellness but also to survival… 'difficulty maintaining self-esteem, and maladaptive efforts to do so, may be central to a variety of mental health problems.' Indeed, when self-esteem is too much of a concern relative to other needs, this is an indication that one's self-esteem has become unhealthy—highly insecure, unstable, and highly dependent on the validation of others."[3]

This external orientation makes the suffering of ignorance a tricky thing. The unwanted, uncontrollable, and unbearable aspects of ignorance remain hidden as the lingering sufferings of fear and shame can be so loud that the need for esteem, even as it emerges, goes unrecognized. Distracted by the external world with its delights and its disasters, we unconsciously allow ignorance to quietly release its influence over our minds; hence the reason we share the euphemism "ignorance is bliss." When we suffer ignorance, the unmet need for self-esteem, we don't necessarily know we are suffering.

Living unconscious to the vast capabilities of being human is like being a fish unable to recognize the water. Unfortunately, there is no formal training of the mind, much less one where we learn what it means to be human. Following the legacy of the Cartesian split, most of our Western minds have been primarily molded by our religious traditions carried into the value systems of our families where parents lend their senses of self to their children until their own is adequately developed. Once again reinforcing our social natures, it is a rare thing to see "the water" without a guide, teacher, or elder pointing out the obvious.[4]

When highlighting the importance of adult guides dedicated to fostering self-discovery in a community's younger members, it is also crucial to acknowledge that many adults are underresourced to offer the proper guidance. In a cycle of unmet needs, many adults never received the necessary guidance to capitalize on their own potentiality of esteem. Self-discovery is left to rely on external validation, leaving them stuck in a state of partial independence or codependence throughout much of their lives.

With readily abundant and accessible sensory distraction found in external validation, ignorance leads to maladaptive behaviors that unknowingly haunt people's lives and corrode their relationships, leaving much of ignorance's burden of suffering to be inflicted upon others. Blissfully unaware, in the underdevelopment of and misidentification with a false sense of self, we cling to a more palatable story of "I," functioning on autopilot, seeing the world through a lens that is blind to the richness life has to offer.[5] Without proper guidance and relationships, we learn to ignore the more nuanced messages of our body-mind, and in ignoring our own feelings and sensations, we are barred from being in full relationship to self and, as consequence, others, especially our children.

As adults, we can recognize and revisit our healthy friendships, mentorships, and intimates to foster the continued development of our self, tending to our ignorance and addressing the need for esteem. Gaining a new perspective, often through acquiring knowledge about the human body-mind and applying it to one's own direct experiences, can enhance one's sense of agency. This newfound understanding empowers individuals to effect meaningful change in their lives, those they are connected to, and the world around them.

Agency is rooted in the prepotency of the mattering established in satisfying our need for connection, understanding our attachments, and seeing ourselves relative to others. Fundamentally, as we move from dependence to independence, the satisfaction of belonging is received and directed inward, strengthening the self as a separate and distinct entity from our families of origin. The need for esteem and the suffering of ignorance then motivate us to know and belong to ourselves.

ESTEEM: WHO AM I?

The greatest scientific discovery was the discovery of ignorance. Once humans realized how little they knew about the world, they suddenly had a very good reason to seek new knowledge, which opened up the scientific road to progress.

— YUVAL NOAH HARARI, *SAPIENS*

Whether trapped on the hedonic treadmill of external consumption, wrapped up in our own emotions, or brandishing one's entitlement, the suffering of ignorance blindly stunts us in our development as humans. We simply forget who and what we really are. The age-old inquiry of "Who Am I?" affords us a glimpse into the experience of self relative to other, and the maturing self can begin to recognize and lean into the suffering of ignorance, expressing the unconscious need to seek the knowledge in order to understand itself.

However, as we have already been alluding to, many of us are completely ignorant to our basic psychology. The human brain is a complex system, and when you begin talking about the manifestation of the mind as an emergent property of said complex system, most people's eyes glaze over with an unspoken message of "you gotta be kidding me!" So, when I work with patients struggling with the suffering of ignorance, I typically focus on two key phenomena essential to mind and the experienced sense of self—the two-system basis of thinking and the multiplicity of mind.

The sense of self is primarily formulated by two systems of thinking, one rooted in our older brains and one from the new. As Nobel Laureate Daniel Kahneman describes in his book entitled, *Thinking, Fast and Slow,* these two systems are one of "unconscious influence" and the other of "conscious deliberation."[6]

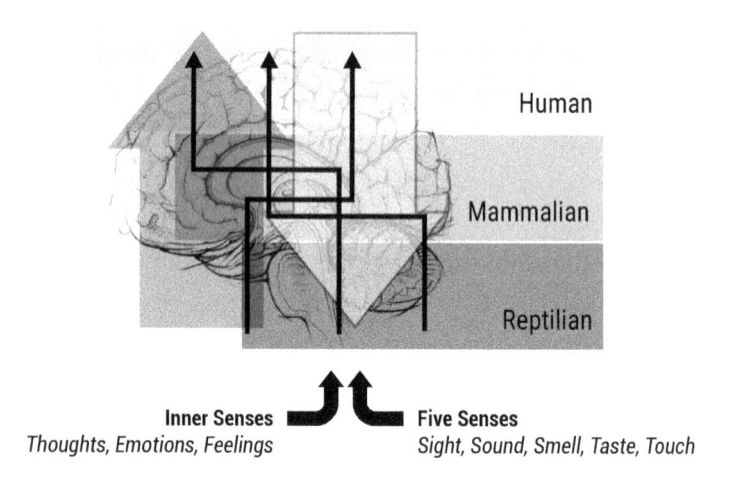

Human

Mammalian

Reptilian

Inner Senses
Thoughts, Emotions, Feelings

Five Senses
Sight, Sound, Smell, Taste, Touch

The "unconscious influence" comes from our more ancient layers of the brain, named by Kahneman as System 1. Fast with endless power, the unconscious thrives on experiential thinking, on feeling. Working from the bottom up, it is irrational, instinctual, and impulsive.

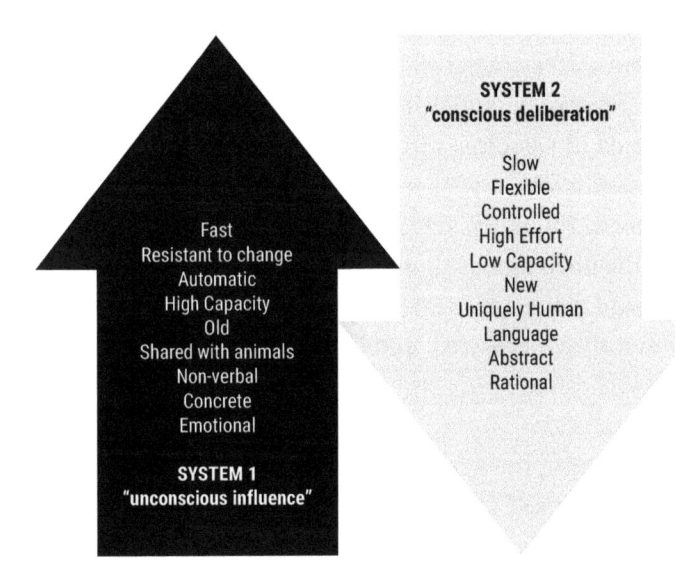

SYSTEM 2
"conscious deliberation"
Slow
Flexible
Controlled
High Effort
Low Capacity
New
Uniquely Human
Language
Abstract
Rational

Fast
Resistant to change
Automatic
High Capacity
Old
Shared with animals
Non-verbal
Concrete
Emotional

SYSTEM 1
"unconscious influence"

Our system of "conscious deliberation" is the newer of the two systems. Uniquely human, this top-down system is the closest thing we can scientifically call the "I" we experience moment to moment. Slow and limited in its power, System 2 is focused on rational thinking, as it likes reasoning and language.

Systems 1 and 2 are home to our subpersonalities and, together, ultimately shape the sense of self.[7]

When oriented inward in what is called the default mode, the brain demonstrates a self-referential state of reflection in the cacophony of our inner dialogue. The default mode allows us to build mental models of our past and imagined futures. When oriented outward in a task positive, goal-oriented stance, the brain receives and sequentially processes incoming sensory information, typically, the core networks fire their regulatory, relational, and reward interpretations, initially eliciting the reactive and gushing power of System 1. System 2 works as a narrowing valve to System 1, with its top-down, responsive, and deliberate nature. However, System 2 is limited in its power and can frequently be overwhelmed by System 1 where we become flooded with a plethora of emotions, thoughts, sensations, and feelings rushing in from the unconscious. Inner conflict, cognitive dissonance, decision fatigue, inertia, and compromise of willpower are commonly experienced, and in extremes cases, self-harm and psychosis are possible.[8]

By addressing the need for esteem, the rational System 2 strengthens itself and learns to open itself more and more to the unknown depths of the emotive System 1, affording us an upward spiraling, integrated sense of self. System 1 thrives on experiential thinking, on feeling, and is able to make wild associations, and with System 2's permissiveness, these wild associations give rise to insights, intuition, and profound creativity, all hallmarks of a self-actualized life.[9]

The crux to developing esteem and broadening the understanding of "I" lies in recognizing the multiplicity of mind. In the 1980s, family therapist Dr. Richard Schwartz, while working with individuals experiencing bulimia, developed Internal Family Systems (IFS), often referred to as "parts" therapy. Directly challenging the long-standing mono-mind theory of psychology, IFS operates on the premise that the *context* of the mind is established in the Self (self with a capital S) who leads the *content* of mind filled with parts or subpersonalities.

The Self of IFS is a direct example of the growing integrations of science and spirituality. Separate from the parts, Self is described as the "inner serenity...the unharmed...inner essence of the mind, the core of who [we are]." Self, shared and consistently exhibited across all humans, displays the qualities of "curiosity, compassion, calm, confidence, clarity, creativity, courage, and connectedness."[10] As it pertains to suffering, the Self is the spirit examined in the upcoming section on the being needs of intimacy and purpose.

Returning to the discussion of subpersonalities, parts—the constant flux of content in the mind—arise in consequence to the experiences of our past, particularly those in childhood, that threatened our safety and survival. Burdened with responsibilities, sensations, and emotions that we were ill-equipped to tolerate, parts hold on to historical narratives and prediction models created to maintain homeostasis within those difficult experiences. Using both thinking systems, parts take control of our sense of self, signal the unmet needs of our past, and powerfully indicate our present-day sufferings. In the words of Schwartz and his colleague, Robert Falconer, in *Many Minds, One Self*:

> "if you consider these interacting components of the mind to be transient, ephemeral thoughts with little power or autonomy, it makes sense to try to help people ignore them...or to counter or correct

the irrational things they say. But if, instead, you consider them to be permanent inner residents of the mind with full-range inner personalities as well as abundant intelligence, autonomy, and power, and if you think they contain many valuable qualities and resources…you [can] listen to them with genuine curiosity and respect, and relate to them in a compassionate, loving way."[11]

The why and how of multiplicity still remain a mystery, but they are likely related to the relationship of the organizational hierarchy of our three-part brain, the core networks, and the two hemispheres that we will discuss further in the suffering of judgment. Regardless, parts and their ability to be led by the Self are what modern psychologists refer to when we talk about the sense of self. The need for esteem calls us to work through the suffering of ignorance to gain the knowledge that subpersonalities exist and begin to appreciate the thinking they do for us.

While I understood the multiplicity of mind in theory and frequently encountered evidence of it in patient care, I was ignorant to the depth of its expression in my own life. Like many people, I was baffled to the power of habits and their impacts on my body-mind. My exposure to the multiplicity of mind has significantly helped me to understand parts and how to lovingly address things like stubborn eating habits, boredom, and other frustrating sensations and emotions that arise on any given day. However, the all-consuming, complicated grief following my dad's death gave me a more direct knowledge of the power of multiplicity, the Self, and the parts most influential in my life.

In the wake of his suicide, my mind was harnessed by what I now know to be a twelve-year-old part named Jenny. She completely overtook the seat of my consciousness, blending to mask the influence of the Self. In what some would call a post-traumatic stress-like response, my body reflected her tastes (Oreos), reading habits (cue YA dystopian binge reading), and ever-present indignation toward my mother (outbursts of preteen rage). Although the now-mature version of me still loves Oreos on occasion and will dive deeply into a book written by Susan Collins or any of her wannabes, I am rarely prone to fits of rage. With enough experience of Self, due to my meditation practice, I recognized Jenny as a protector part calling my attention. It seemed Jenny was activated to run an old program of defense, as a more vulnerable part was feeling threatened.

In IFS, injured parts are called Exiles. Exiles are protected by Managers and Firefighters. Managers are proactive parts that usually play by some set of rules, and Firefighters are reactive parts, and to them, survival is the only rule of the game.[12] We all have this experience. In cartoons, it's the angel on one shoulder and the devil on the other bickering with you in between. Jenny was definitely a Firefighter committed to dousing the flames of a perceived danger.

As the oldest of four children, born to teenage parents, I assumed significant household responsibilities very early in my life. By the age of twelve, I was actively managing the destabilizing and polarizing forces of my mother's emotional immaturity and my father's need to maintain an external image of control and wealth. Forced to prematurely take on adult roles while maintaining an air of competence and poise,

I had contorted myself into a picture of precociousness that was not only valued but rewarded by the adults surrounding me, especially my parents. At this point in my history, Jenny assumed this burden and asserted herself in my psyche.

Jenny was likely the internal force that gave me the strength to leave home at seventeen and create a life of my own. Once my independence was solid and the burdens of my family of origin no longer threatened my life, Jenny receded to the depths of my inner life. Though it would be nearly four decades later, Jenny's burden returned, reactivated by the deluge of responsibilities that come with a traumatic and unexpected death of a parent.

Through IFS therapy, massage, and deep meditation, I learned to openly receive the overwhelming experience of the burden Jenny had carried all these years. Building tolerance to the vulnerability of childhood neglect, Self was able to assert a bit of space, and Jenny's programming was allowed to quiet. In the brief moments of quiet, the Exile Jenny was protecting was revealed and the system of parts protecting the Exile that included Jenny was unburdened from the past and integrated into my life in the present.

Jenny, finally unburdened, was able to take on a role more suited to her tenacity and resourcefulness. It seems the Exile Jenny was protecting was an infant named Olive who was burdened with all the basic needs my child-self was not able to express. Now, in the present, I honor Jenny and Olive by ensuring that my basic needs are always attended to and satisfied.

I share this not as a "should" but more as a way of providing narrative instruction to the growing science in the multiplicity and thinking theories of mind. This also gives you an idea of the road ahead. Actively plumbing the dark recesses of our mind is a task for the sufferings of spirit that requires tolerance to vulnerability rooted in the satisfactions of the self, knowledge, and curiosity. Without right perspective and agency, we navigate life with the blindness of ignorance, and our developmental travels stall, leaving us stuck in the loop of self-perpetuated suffering.

GAINING PERSPECTIVE

...we are hopelessly absorbed with ourselves... When you combine natural narcissism with the basic need for self-esteem, you create a creature who has to feel himself an object of primary value: first in the universe, representing in himself all of life...[yet], it is all the more curious how ignorant most of us are, consciously, of what we really want and need...

— ERNEST BECKER, *THE DENIAL OF DEATH*

Ignorance and its consequential psychological entropy thrive on what seems to be an external locus of control, and the people who are suffering the unmet need of self-esteem live at the whims of sensations, emotions, feelings, and thoughts. Often working in tandem with shame, ignorance compromises the foundational connection to the rudimentary sense of self. In his beautiful book, *The Wild Edge of Sorrow,* author Francis Weller poignantly captures this sentiment:

"...our one-dimensional obsession with emotional progress...places enormous pressure on us to always be improving, feeling good, and rising above our problems. Happiness has become the new mecca, and anything short of that often leaves us feeling that we have done something wrong or failed to live up to the acknowledged standard. This forces sorrow, pain, fear, weakness, and vulnerability into the underworld, where they fester and mutate into contorted expressions of themselves, often coated in a mantle of shame."[13]

Grasping and clinging to external sources of validation and soothing results in relapsing and remitting "only ifs," or what psychologists call the "hedonic treadmill." Originally proposed in the early seventies, the hedonic treadmill theory states that "people briefly react to good and bad events, but in a short time they return to neutrality. Thus, happiness and unhappiness are merely short-lived reactions to changes in people's circumstances. People continue to pursue happiness because they incorrectly believe that greater happiness lies just around the corner in the next goal accomplished, the next social relationship obtained, or the next problem solved. Because new goals continually capture one's attention, one constantly strives to be happy without realizing that in the long run such efforts are futile."[14]

In the never-ending chase for more—more money, more status, more things—there are no winners. As we, quite literally, have lost our senses, many modern societies foster consumption and external validation as the effectual means by which to fortify the sense of self. In the most extreme cases of consumption to secure the self, I have seen the ability of addiction to ravage lives. One of the most enlightening pieces of knowledge gleaned during my residency was coming to the understanding that addiction is primarily about the relief of pain. Overwhelmed with the sensations of physical, psychological, or spiritual injury or illness, persons suffer the ignorance of the unmet need for self-esteem and are pushed by the body-mind toward anything that can break the cycle of pain, even if just for a millisecond.

Beautifully yet painfully articulated by mystic J. Krishnamurti: "When there is only one thing in your life that is an avenue to ultimate escape, to complete forgetfulness of yourself if only for a few seconds, you cling to it because that is the only moment you are happy…"[15]

Reflecting the importance of gaining perspective, growing tolerant to the onslaught of senses, and welcoming the Self leadership of parts, Krishnamurti continues with, "If we have no beliefs with which the mind had identified itself, then the mind, without identification, is capable of looking at itself as it is—and then, surely, there is the beginning of the understanding of oneself."[16]

Tolerance of sensory input rests in prepotent satisfaction of our survival needs where we learn prediction and pause to foster attention and healthy attachment. From this safe and secure base, we can learn to further embody and welcome sensory experiences at their gates, gaining perspective. Each of our sense gates can be used in three ways in what I call *passive reception, active reception,* and *open reception.*

Take smell—from right where you are in this moment, what smells are coming at you? For me, I am currently in a bakery and am passively bombarded by the odors of coffee, tea, sugar, cinnamon, and dough. Next, take a deep whiff of the air. Can you smell anything else? If I purposefully pick up the sense of smell, I actively gain a few more layers of odor—the furniture polish used to clean the tables, the perfume of the woman sitting at the table next to me, and the sulfur of cooked eggs. If I close my eyes and rest back into an open state of receptivity, smell shifts from a nose-based gate to a Self-oriented experience where smell is known through the body-mind as a whole. The experience is hard to articulate, but it is pretty wild. Try this with all of your external senses.

The internal senses—feeling, emotion, and thoughts—are registered at the gates of the gut, heart, and brain, respectively. Interception, the ability to sense and tolerate internal information is where most of us fall short. When we are overwhelmed by these messages, we tend to repress or avoid them—frequently stuffing, hiding, or drugging them. We can also be confused with our feelings, emotions, and thoughts, like when we are simultaneously overstimulated yet equally bored. These internal senses are foundational to survival needs and self needs, especially in the establishment of agency and the satisfaction of esteem. These internal queues motivate us and allow us to persist against frustration, to delay gratification, to regulate moods, to hope, and to control impulse.[17]

The same exercise of passive receptivity, active receptivity, and open receptivity can be applied to the streams of internal senses as well. Try thought—close your eyes and just note, what thoughts are vying for your attention? Note the machinations of System 1 and System 2? For me, it's a fog of heat and fatigue with a paradoxically pervasive pleasant quality. Interspersed are things like wondering how my son is playing on the golf course, what am I going to make for dinner, how am I going to meet my publishing deadline, and it goes on and on. This is not active thinking. The brain just registers thought, like the nose registers smell and our attention gets sucked in.

Now pick up one of those thoughts and actively pursue it. Here's mine: "For dinner, I'll make chicken Caesar salad, because, God knows, I don't want to go to the store if I don't have to." Now, for the last part. Can you let go of valence, recognize and let go of anything salient, and rest back in open receptivity to just let the body-mind experience thought as a stream of unregulated sensory input? From this allowing witness perspective, thoughts, like smells, can flow through uncaptured.

What if we applied this to the sense of self? In this case, the seat of consciousness is the sense gate that registers parts. Some parts claim the seat uninvited. Remember the part that responded to being cut off in traffic earlier? You can also actively invite parts to make themselves known, easing into relationship with Self. From this vantage point, parts are received with calm and compassion. When we take the perspective of open receptivity, the seat is fully claimed by Self, and we rest back with confidence, clarity, and connectedness.

This is true in the other sense experiences as well and can serve as a way to get in touch with the core essence of your existence. To this end, the strength of the sense of self can be worked and molded, just like a sommelier develops and refines her sense of smell. Once we are able to tolerate sensations, our perspective grows, reactivity moves toward responsiveness, and the opportunity to see ourselves fully—our quirky parts, our dark sides, our evils—arises.

The root of our psychological entropy slowly reveals itself, and the promise of healing the body-mind split comes to fruition. This healing allows us to work with our parts to unburden, transform, and incorporate those underdeveloped aspects of ourselves. Shifting the narrow perspective of ignorance to a more realistic and broader view of ourselves enables agency, deeper social connections, empathy for others, and the developing belief in our own social value as an adult member of the community.

AGENCY

…you may not be entitled to shine, but you have the right to shine, because you are a worthy human being. Changing your self-limiting narratives about your worthiness, asserting needs in a healthy way, overcoming your avoidance of fearful experiences, and taking responsibility for your behaviors—these actions strengthen and stabilize the vulnerable self. The great irony is that the less you focus on whether you are worthy and competent, and take that as a given, the greater the chances you will consistently accept your inherent worth.
— SCOTT BARRY KAUFMAN, *TRANSCEND*

First articulated by Maslow and updated by Kaufman, our need for esteem manifests in two ways:

The first is about mastery:

"*Are you an intentional being who can bring about your desired goals by exercising your will?*"

The second relates to personal value:

"*Are you a fundamentally good person with social value in this world?*"[18]

Mastery is the self-knowledge rooted in the identification and fostering of one's constitution and capabilities. Learning to effectively "play the cards you've been dealt" gives rise to agency—our ability to act independently, make choices, and have the power to influence the direction of our lives. Agency grows with the integration of our two thinking systems, the unburdening of parts, and the continued exercise of our capabilities. From effective agency, mastery evolves.[19]

Gaining perspective creates the circumstances for agency to materialize, as it makes room for an honest inquiry into who one is. With right perspective, we can begin to take a simple stock of our genetics and epigenetics (the genetic impact of our family history), qualities of personality, talents, and skills. We begin to build the self-knowledge needed to appreciate the conceptual difference between self and other and how this translates into our current perception of the world. Using Assagioli's framework of subpersonalities, we can delve a little further into agency:

- What do I believe myself to be?
- What would I like to be?

- How do I believe others see me?
- What do I want to appear to be?
- What do I believe I can become?[20]

According to Scott Barry Kaufman, "the latest research suggests that a healthy self-esteem is an outcome of genuine accomplishment and intimate connection with others, and of a sense of growing and developing as a whole person." He further substantiates this with the statement that "self-esteem is one of the strongest correlates of life satisfaction."[21]

Maslow and other of his contemporaries also believed esteem is about personal power. A secure esteem "is associated with real strength and earned confidence." He also believed those with secure sense of self have "high self-respect, and evaluation of self; a feeling of being able to handle other people; a feeling of mastery; a feeling that others do and ought to admire and respect one; a feeling of general capability; an absence of shyness, timidity, self-consciousness, or embarrassment; and a feeling of pride." Maslow goes on to state that those with insecure self-esteem overcompensate with "with antagonism to others, willfulness, impoliteness, selfishness, aggressiveness, tyrannizing…snobbishness, haughty, [and] cold…interested not so much in helping weaker people as in dominating them and hurting them."[22]

Accordingly, conversations of agency and power also raise the questions of sexuality. With its vast and far-reaching implications to human development, sex is a charged and often polarizing topic. Maslow, though controversially, did discuss sexuality. He asserted sexuality took on two faces, one originating from "drive," where sex was related to satisfying deficiency needs, and the other from growth, described as "dominance." The inflection point between these two faces is reflected in the adequate satisfaction of esteem needs. Maslow's use of dominance and, as consequence, submissive language reflects the heteronormative view of sexuality that pervaded 1930s' society and certainly biased the hierarchy's development.[23]

In my observations, expressions of sexuality are a way to communicate one's unmet needs and rely to a great degree on the tenor of a person's situational suffering, as it relates to survival, self, or spirit. Sexuality expressed to stave off fear and shame often involves conflicts of consent and self-preservation asserted by the arousal pathway of aggression and violence or the dissociation pathway of compliance and capitulation. The sufferings of ignorance and judgment, often indicative of one's culture and society, seemingly raise issues of reproduction, emotional connectivity, gender identity, and sexual preference and desire. Isolation and longing reach into the more qualitative experiences of erotic intelligence, true interdependence, and sexual spirituality. Though it may be surprising to some, in my practice, discussions of a person's sexual life often reveal the true nature of their suffering.

KNOWLEDGE
Real knowledge is to know the extent of one's ignorance.
—CONFUCIUS

We are timebound creatures, subject to change. In clinging to or avoiding this absolute, we suffer ignorance. Nowhere more in our lives does this play out than in our experience of self.

The working knowledge of our mind—its sense of self, its binary modalities of thinking, and its multiplicity—transformed by the choice to gain perspective, not only offers up the developmental faculty of agency and the experiences of mastery and social value, but it also affords us the abilities to self-regulate and "accept the ownership of our feelings and actions."[24]

With our attention and attachments under our agent command, we are readied to learn and engage, orchestrating the development of an "authentic voice."[25] Reinforced by mastery, current life choices are perceived to have direct impact on one's future self, and as Kaufman states, the satisfaction of self-knowledge gives us "coherence and hope."[26]

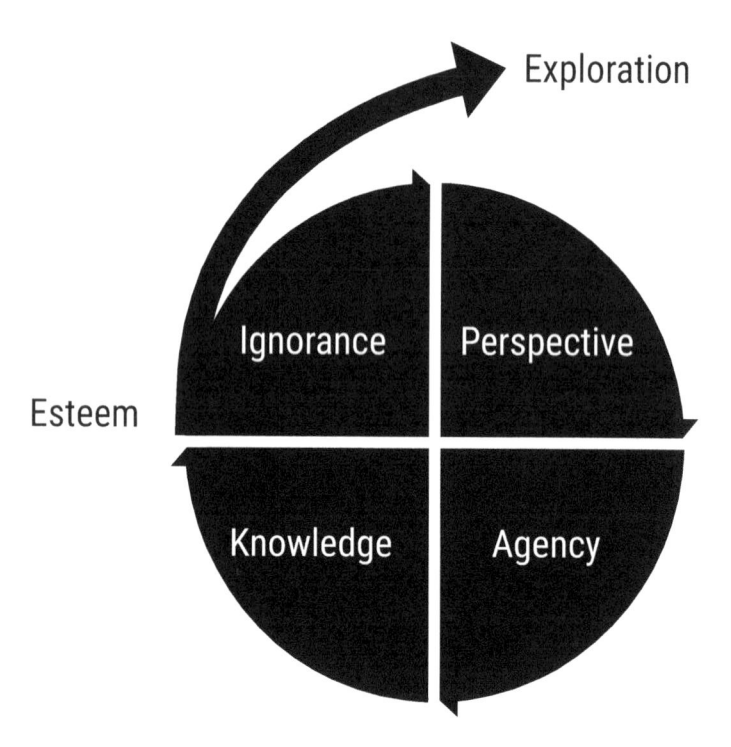

From the satisfaction of esteem, the need for exploration emerges, where we are called to make use of the knowledge we have gained to travel further in our worlds, both internally and externally.

The unmet need for exploration leads to the suffering of judgment. So, as Brené Brown gently reminds us, "Knowledge is important, but only if we're being kind and gentle with ourselves as we work to discover who we are."[27]

Judgment.

As long as we see our suffering as evidence of worthlessness, we will not move toward our wounds with anything but judgment.
—FRANCIS WELLER, WILD EDGE OF SORROW

If you find yourself on this page, I salute you. It takes a brave soul to bear the discomfort that comes with knowledge of how complex we are as creatures. Judgment, usually driven by the prepotent sufferings of fear and shame, can quickly drive a hand to slam a book shut when it reads about multiplicity, the seat of consciousness, or the fortitude of our ancient brains. Sometimes, the tension between what you wish it to be and what it actually is can be so great that all you can do is just sit with a glass of wine and doomscroll for hours on end, ignoring any external or internal signals, all in hopes of a blissful, numbing distraction. Collapsed by the weight of it all, the "f*ckits" kick in and you're just left with a blob of a mind and a blown feeling of something that should be but isn't. Sound familiar?

Remember the earlier comment about development feeling very herky-jerky—one step forward, two steps back? The shift from the sufferings of survival to the sufferings of the self is one of those herky-jerky moments, especially as the sense of self strengthens and the need for exploration emerges with the suffering of judgment. In turn, one of the first exercises of exploration is an about-face to revisit the views and beliefs we have about the world, others, and ourselves. As part of that process, we return to our previously satisfied needs to reframe and reload with the knowledge we've gained. In the words of master poet Maya Angelou, invoked by her mentee, Oprah Winfrey: "you did…what you knew how to do, and when you knew better, you did better."[1]

At this great shift, we are at risk to be thwarted by the pitfalls of judgment. Fixated on maintaining control—particularly in the face of fluctuating safety and security needs—many people languish in their development, stagnating at partial independence. Faced with drives and desires from an insecure sense of self, people tend toward one of three paths: indulge, distract, or deny.

Indulging judgments, we are quick to compare, compete, or condemn, stifling our curiosity and hampering our willingness to grow. Judgment-driven suffering is inherently self-centered, as one's sense of worth is tied to comparisons and the need to be perceived as "better" than others. A life steeped in comparison fosters beliefs and values rooted in vanity, envy, and hate. Blinded by ambition, competition ensues, pitting us against the world. And, when our self-identity is weaponized to wield upon others who pose a threat to its existence, condemnation engenders prejudice and disgust. In all cases, our exercise of agency becomes limited to self-oriented activities, leading to minimal meaningful service or interaction and rendering us oblivious to the suffering of others. This diminishes our appreciation of relational rewards, and personal growth is blunted.

To distract from judgment, instincts and impulses become weapons of self-destruction. Multitasking and overconsumption lead to unproductive busyness, greed, lust, and gluttony, numb our suffering, and blunt our ability to meet our essential needs. As energy is diverted to meeting our wants, pleasure is used to overshadow pain. The necessary pain of enduring, striving, and learning gets lost in the fray, and though we may appear to "have it all," reality says we are anxious and addicted, burned-out and bloated.

Wanting and desire are essential to the experience of life. As Daniel Lieberman, states: "desire may be viewed as a primitive emotion, reflecting our animal nature, but without desire, we can't make intellectual sense of the world, because assigning value to a thing is an essential part of understanding it."[2] This is why boredom is such an uncomfortable feeling. So, when judgment is denied, suffering takes the shape of anhedonia—the place where nothing is salient, and nothing satisfies. Depressed, people become inert with no interest in meeting their needs.

These words may ring with the language of biblical fire and brimstone, and that is likely true. Our faith traditions incorporate some of the best language to describe suffering, and living in the Bible Belt, my patients so often use these words to describe its experience. In sharing this with a colleague who is nearing fifty years of service as a nondenominational Christian pastor and hospital chaplain, he articulated one of his greatest worries with: "It seems we have moved from making lifestyle choices to making deathstyle choices, where we have become phat (with a "ph"), dumb, and numb all in the pursuit of being 'happy.' In this pursuit, people seem to lose interest and capacity to navigate the challenges of living."

Especially in the looming reality of death, I have borne witness to the gridlock that judgment brings to patients in their last days, flavoring such a precious time with the sourness of regret in not living life to its fullest. Whether through indulging, distracting, or denying, plagued by judgment, the possibility of actualization is greatly jeopardized.

Author and business thought leader Daniel Pink, in his book *The Power of Regret,* articulates this beautifully:

> "When people tell you their regrets, their enduring regrets, and they're all the same over and over again, they tell you what matters most to them out of life. And one of the things that matters to most of us out of life, is doing something, learning, growing, trying stuff, leading a psychologically rich life, that's who we are."[3]

Regret has the potential to reveal to us what matters most, and it also has the capacity to equally drop us back into disconnection, shame, and even fear. The suffering of judgment, through regret, teaches us the nuanced differences between a life driven to survive relative to one driven to thrive.

This is where our human superpower of agency exudes its most important evolutionary role. The chore of agency is to empower us to grow, but its effectiveness is narrowed when exercised with judgment. Begging the question: Can I consciously make the choice to follow my curiosity, take the risks, embrace the paradoxes of life, and let go of the "me" to aspire to be fully human?

EXPLORATION: AM I WILLING TO GROW?

We are the life-force power of the universe with manual dexterity and two cognitive minds. We have the power to choose, moment by moment, who and how we want to be in the world. Right here, right now, I can step in to the consciousness of my right hemisphere, where we are, I am...at One with all that is. Or, I can choose to step in to the consciousness of my left hemisphere, where I become a single individual...separate from the flow. These are the "We" inside of me. Which do you choose...and when?

— JILL BOLTE TAYLOR, *WHOLE BRAIN LIVING*

Once we are adequately satisfied in our first three needs, the need for exploration emerges, signaling the call to integrate the various aspects of our identity. In first honoring the basic needs for safety and connection, we become aware of the functioning self. And when the need for esteem opens to knowledge, we are then invited to explore the self's structure to further reveal the path toward actualization.

The human part of the brain is dissimilar to the reptilian and mammalian parts in that it has a bias toward growth and creativity and seeks to take calculated risks in order to learn and explore. The need for exploration calls us toward direct experience to reinforce the knowledge we have gained. If instinct, impulsivity, and imperative drive the reptilian and mammalian brains, then intention drives the human brain. Fostering the necessary opening to the unconscious, we shift from a binary view of pleasure and pain to a paradoxical view where both can be fully present in each situation. But in paradox we often face conflicting developmental goals, and in this paradoxical tension, the need for exploration drives us from the suffering of judgment to the satisfaction of curiosity.

In the spirit of exploration, let's return to our investigation of the human brain. Adding to the anatomy and physiology of the three—human, mammalian, and reptilian—layers, the brain also has two hemispheres. Independent yet interconnected, the right and left hemispheres are the basis of the "we inside me" concept made famous by neuroscientist Jill Bolte Taylor. In her book, *Whole Brain Living,* Bolte Taylor details the hemispheres of the human brain:

> "At any moment in time, both hemispheres have cells that are active, but opposing hemisphere cell groups dance between dominance and inhibition. In this way, one hemisphere has the power to inhibit the function of the comparable cells in the opposite hemisphere, dominating the function of the particular group of cells. For example, when we are focused on the words and meaning of what someone is saying (left brain), we tend to not be so focused on the inflection of their voice or the emotional content (right brain)

of what they are communicating. Vice versa—have you ever been so stunned that someone was yelling at you that you completely missed the point they were trying to make?"[4]

Debunking the left-right brain craze of the 1970s and '80s, a consequence of studies done on people with split brains, Bolte Taylor goes on discuss the science demonstrating how "Both of our cerebral hemispheres are constantly contributing to the whole of any experiential moment." While these findings are conclusively true, each hemisphere displays unique functional expertise based on the way neurons in each hemisphere deal with information.

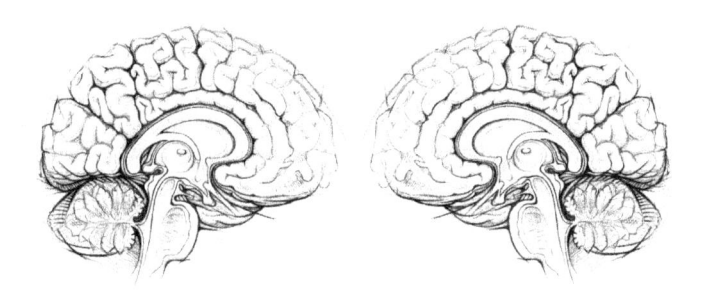

Getting to the heart of it, Bolte Taylor continues, "The neurons in our left brain function linearly: they take an idea to the next idea, and then compare the by-product of those ideas to the *next* idea…whereby we can separate past, present, and future. Our right-brain cells are not at all designed to create linear order. Instead, our right hemisphere functions like a parallel processor, bringing in multiple streams of data that simultaneously… manifest a rich composite of right here, right now present moment by adding depth to the creation of our memories, which are influenced by both of our hemispheres."[5]

Even more mind-boggling, when coupled with the bimodal thinking discussed earlier—the two systems of "unconscious influence" and "conscious deliberation"—our two hemispheres create four unique systems of thinking. As further detailed in the diagram:

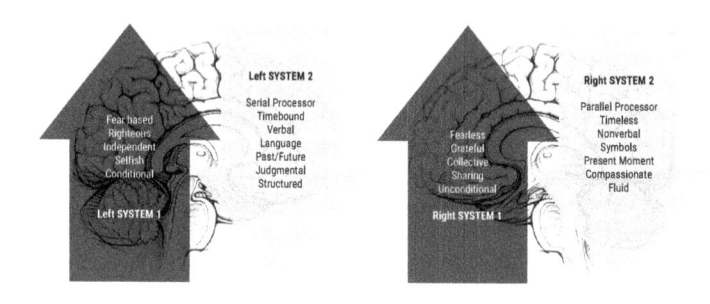

[Diagram: Left SYSTEM 2 — Serial Processor, Timebound, Verbal, Language, Past/Future, Judgmental, Structured; Left SYSTEM 1 — Fear based, Righteous, Independent, Selfish, Conditional. Right SYSTEM 2 — Parallel Processor, Timeless, Nonverbal, Symbols, Present Moment, Compassionate, Fluid; Right SYSTEM 1 — Fearless, Grateful, Collective, Sharing, Unconditional]

- Left System 1 "feels and knows our past pain…[and] the boundaries of [one's] safety…and is preoccupied with…fear."
- Left System 2 thinks linearly and top-down to serve as our "goal driven…judge…[of] right/wrong, good/bad." It thrives on order.
- Right System 1, like its left counterpart, is focused on safety from the standpoint of familiarity. However, it is focused in the here and now and on novelty and having fun. In Bolte Taylor's words, "It [acts] impulsively in the present moment without considering the consequences of our behavior."
- Right System 2 is, according to Bolte Taylor, "the part of our brain that *is* a spiritual being having a physical experience." It is the home of our spirit.[6]

Consequently, at any given time, depending on circumstance, each system can take over the seat of consciousness to address the issue at hand.

Although this science is still emerging, hopefully this helps to understand where the multiplicity of mind comes from and piques your interest to explore its many faces. Even more, I hope the knowledge encourages you to be interested in the seat of consciousness—the basis of our spirit, the Self with a capital S—the focus of the next section of the book. Whetting your appetite further, "Consciousness is unlike any other product of natural selection. Consciousness [opens] our eyes, allowing us to see beyond mere survival and reproduction. It [allows] us to transcend our biological roots, giving us the ability to contemplate higher things, such as justice, beauty, and truth."[7] In contemplation, we get glimpses into the potentialities of actualization, and in these glimpses, we are drawn to know more. "Who am I?" becomes "Who am I, *really*?" which prompts a stalwart readiness in asking *"Am I willing to grow?"*

Adding flavor to the willingness to grow question, Scott Barry Kaufman, in his blog *Beautiful Minds,* offers a simple self-inquiry that drills further into the need for exploration:

1. Are you interested in activities that will expand your horizons?
2. Do you think it's important to have new experiences that challenge how you think about yourself and the world?
3. Do you feel as though you have really improved yourself as a person over the years?

4. Do you have the sense that you have developed a lot as a person over time?
5. Do you enjoy being in new situations that require you to change your old familiar ways of doing things?
6. Has life been a continuous process of learning, changing, and growth for you?[8]

Active human development is a foundational element of our primary education system, but beyond elementary school, no system cross-sectionally exists to encourage our ongoing development. Despite this formal demarcation in education, we continue to develop throughout the entirety of our lives. So, regardless of age, a mindset of continued growth reinforced by purposeful activities of development is essential to an actualized life.

Shaped significantly by the prepotent satisfactions of stability, belonging, and knowledge, the need for exploration is best reflected in the work of research psychologists Richard Ryan and Edward Deci. Termed Self-Determination Theory (SDT), Ryan and Deci's research discusses this necessity of intentional activity to foster development across the lifespan. SDT recognizes the sufferings of judgment by calling out the human "inclination toward activity and integration, but also...[the] vulnerability to passivity."[9] Consequently, SDT names three cornerstones in the foundation of its theory: relatedness, competence, and autonomy:

> *Relatedness*, stemming from our need for connection is "perhaps the most pervasive and powerful force that controls behavior, as people are highly motivated to be recognized or loved by others."

Competency "is defined as individuals' inherent desire to feel effective in interacting with the environment. It is prominent in the propensity to explore and manipulate the environment and to engage in challenging tasks to test and extend one's skills. Competence satisfaction allows individuals to adapt to complex and changing environments, whereas competence frustration is likely to result in helplessness and a lack of motivation."

Autonomy is a little more nuanced. While not synonymous with independence, autonomy relates to a spectrum of ability to exercise personal agency, choice, and will. Per Deci and Ryan, "autonomy is characterized by integrative processing of possibilities and a matching of these with sensibilities, needs, and constraints."[10]

Arguing that the "centrality of motivation in human function" goes much further than the simplicity of reward circuitry of the brain, Deci and Ryan articulate another set of dichotomies—the two primary human motivations: external, pressured and internal, autonomous. Ryan and Deci substantiate the externally, controlled oriented issues of judgment—indulgence, distraction, and denial—"can actually taint a person's feelings about…basic worth…and undermine intrinsic motivation." To this point, their work can be summarized: "Accumulated research now suggests that commitment and authenticity reflected in intrinsic motivation and integrated extrinsic motivation are most likely to be evident when individuals experience support for competence, autonomy and relatedness." SDT shows us that integration is the key to flipping the judgment triad on its head, transforming indulgence, distraction, and denial into relatedness, competence, and autonomy.[11]

Our nature is inherently "*paradoxical...*[it] is half animal and half symbolic."[12] Integration is contingent upon our agency and willingness to grow. Judgment calls us to shift perspective from externally driven to internally authentic, to attend the unconscious and plumb its vast possibilities,

and to marry the left and right of our existence. However, to do this, we must learn to tolerate the tension of our natural paradox.

HOLDING PARADOX

Know how sublime a thing it is to suffer and be strong.
— HENRY WADSWORTH LONGFELLOW

The suffering of judgment comes from the universal condition of paradox. The tension of duality coupled with cycles of change create circumstances where we must hold two conflicting truths simultaneously. Paradox often sits at the heart of risk-taking, where judgment clamps down our curiosity in an effort to maintain a safe, secure sense of self.

When paradox is held, cherished even, the suffering of judgment pushes us to explore, and aspiration is made visible. Exercising the power of paradox to spark the flame of aspiration quiets the interference of judgment and gives us the bravery to turn inward to plumb the depths of the world inside. Our inherent curiosity then guides us in discovering what truly matters to us in this lifetime. Here we begin to glimpse the more subtle, truer element of our existence. As the Cartesian split of the body-mind begins to heal and our parts integrate, our relational experiences initiate the development of rudimentary values and beliefs, ethics and morals, finding some roadmap to navigate life. Beyond the body-mind and the expression of self, our core consciousness slowly reveals itself. Becoming moves to being, independence moves to interdependence, and transcendence becomes possible.

Exploration is essential to the integration of the paradox of the two-system mind. As experts have noted, the only way to modify the bottom-up system is through direct experience. Given the unconscious speaks through feeling, sensation, emotion, and symbolic language, no wonder we are drawn to works of art and the wonders of nature. You can look at every picture captured of the great redwoods, the northern lights, the Sistine Chapel, or the Venus de Milo, but one must directly encounter such creations to appreciate their captivating capacities and the profound power they have to call to the extraordinary aspects of us humans.[13]

The most meaningful art is unafraid of the both/and, displaying the entirety of direct experience. In what is known as the "terrible sublime," art is a living example of holding paradox. As German philosopher Immanuel Kant eloquently articulated in his *Critique of Judgment,* he agrees with Edmund Burke's conceptualization of the sublime: "'[It] rests on the impulse toward self-preservation and on fear, i.e. on a pain... not indeed pleasure, but a kind of satisfying horror, a certain tranquility tinged with terror.'"[14] For a taste, just listen to the bittersweet music of Leonard Cohen, read Paul Bloom and his thoughts on "pleasurable pain," or watch Alyssa Monks's TED Talk on the "beautiful awful."[15]

When we confront the terrible two-system mind and begin to explore the depths of our unconscious, we encounter the sublime within.

But such exploration requires tolerance to risk. Here, we can learn something from our children. "Kids will take a chance," as Sir Ken Robinson said in his highly viewed 2006 TED Talk. He goes on to say, "They're not frightened of being wrong.… If you're not prepared to be wrong, you'll never come up with anything original.… And by the time they get to be adults, most kids have lost that capacity. They have become frightened of being wrong." Highlighting the high cost of our society's emphasis on the rational, conscious mind, Robinson continues: "And we run our companies like this. We stigmatize mistakes… Truthfully, what happens is, as children grow up, we start to educate them progressively from the waist up. And then we focus on their heads. And slightly to one side."[16]

On a similar note, when I am teaching health-profession students about the power of laying hands when caring for the sick and the dying, I intentionally call out the tendency for students to develop what I call the "Good Will Hunting" syndrome. As you might recall, in the movie of the same name, we follow Will, a young man graced with the gift of an eidetic memory. He can recall the finest of details of photos or nuances of readings his mind has been exposed to, but the experiences are indirect, two-dimensional, and impersonal. It is not until he engages in the fullness of life's experience, directly, does he truly begin living.[17] Similarly, students find safety in reading about their patients' diseases, becoming comfortably proficient in the language of pathology, but when pressed to tell me the color of their patients' eyes, or the smell of their cancer, or the feel of their pulse, or the tenor of emotion pervading the room, most sheepishly recoil within the safe, abstract, rational knowledge of their textbooks and computer screens.

Each set of needs exemplify paradox in and of themselves. Reflected in pairs of sufferings, the more prepotent selfish need underpins its more socially oriented counterpart. Safety is prepotent to the social need for connection, esteem is necessary for exploration, intimacy required for purpose. Holding paradox requires we effectively exercise prediction, pause, and perception to wrangle judgment toward curiosity.

Holding paradox requires intention. Using the more top-down parts of our hemispheres, intention helps the conscious to find interest in the unconscious imperatives, impulses, and instincts. Returning to Buddhist psychologist Jack Kornfield, "Be mindful of intention. Intention is the seed that creates our future…from intention springs deed, from the deed spring the habits. From the habits grow the character, from character develops destiny… Take care not to mix intention with delusion."[18]

I offer a simple but not easy exercise of holding paradox to invoke intentionality in your life. The exercise explores your life from the imaginary lens of your death:

- Practice Prediction: Prepare, Be Present
    - Prepare: Grab a blank sheet of paper and a pen.
    - Be Present: Find a quiet space where you won't be disturbed for at least thirty minutes.
- Invoke the Pause: HALT, RAIN it in! Address any basic needs.
- Gain Perspective: With a deep breath, close your eyes. Anything in your environment knocking at your sense doors? Begin to actively take notice of each sense experience: external (touch, taste, sight, sound, smell) and internal (feelings, emotions, thoughts). Now shift back to open receptivity, allowing sensory experiences to flow without interference in the present moment.
- Hold Paradox:
    - Now, gently imagine yourself on your deathbed. Allow the sensory experience to enter your body-mind. Where are you? Who is there, if anyone? Do you notice any specific sights, sounds, smells, tastes, touches? Explore for a few breaths. When you are ready, capture it on the front side of the paper. Draw or narrate as you so choose.
    - When complete, rest back, closing your eyes. Return again to your deathbed. Imagine you are in the last minutes and hours of your life. What thoughts, images, feelings, and emotions are present? What is your heart's deepest desire? Again, explore for a few breaths. When you are ready, turn the page over and on the left side write all the words down to capture what you've witnessed.
    - From this list, circle the five most salient words. The thinking mind will interject, stick with feeling into the words that matter most.

- Now, on the right side of the page, list out the five words starting with the most salient at the top.
- Perform the Postmortem:
    - Ranging from joyful embraces to fearful denials, people approach death and grief in mirror to how they live and emote in life... In looking at this list that represents what you espouse to hold most dear, how do you live these words in your daily life?
    - Where in your life do you have regrets?
- Return to practicing prediction:
    - With this new insight, how will you prepare for tomorrow?
    - Anything you need to do different today?

To close this activity, I share words from a fellow palliative care clinician, Tony Bossis. Tony often uses the Greek word Χαρμολύπη (charmolypi), pronounced HAR-mo-lippi, to relay this paradox of a death-informed life. Χαρμολύπη translates to "joyful sorrow," "sweet sorrow," "joy-filled mourning," or "tears of blood."[19]

ASPIRATION

...the sublime, the beautiful, and the divine are inextricable from basic animal functions...
— ERNEST BECKER, *THE DENIAL OF DEATH*

In rectifying our own paradoxical experience, aspiration erupts. All great acts begin with a hope, a dream, an aspiration. Through the above exercise, intention is crafted in the use of aspirational imagination, a uniquely human function where we are safe to explore the unknown. Aspiration leads to intention, which leads to action. Creating the story of your life with the end in mind is aspirational, as you now have the map of treasures you will need to gather along the way. The compass of suffering is your guide.

Across our existence as a species, we have written, sculpted, drawn, painted—to tell the great stories, to invoke our faculty of aspiration. We need aspiration to address the sufferings of the spirit. Without it, curiosity collapses. We see evidence of the power of imagination and storytelling to foster aspiration, but we must be careful. Chimamanda Ngozi Adichie at TEDGlobal 2009 poignantly discussed "the [powerful] consequence of the single story." She reminds us of judgment's heavy influence on our imaginations as she states the single story "robs people of dignity… Stories matter… Stories have been used to dispossess and to malign, but stories can also be used to empower and to humanize. Stories can break the dignity of a people, but stories can also repair that broken dignity."[20]

Joseph Campbell's monomyth of the hero's journey, captured in *The Hero with a Thousand Faces,* underpins many, if not most, of our human aspirational tales. The story is a beautiful example of paradox, in that it invokes mythological forces while providing practical pattern recognition of self-directed human development. Mirroring the creation, transformation, dissolution cycle of evolution, the hero's journey first beckons the traveler with its call, asks the traveler to cross a one-way threshold of unknown possibilities, where death and rebirth return the traveler atoned and gifted and wholly new. *Star Wars, Harry Potter, The Wizard of Oz, To Kill a Mockingbird,* or my favorite, *The Alchemist* are just a few stories that model this intrinsically human experience of aspirational development.[21]

Through our imagination and stories we choose to exercise or deny our abilities of aspiration, foster or run fallow curiosity, and bring forth or obstruct the flow of spirit. Returning us to Maslow,

> "If we clearly and fully recognize that these noble and good impulses come into existence and grow potent primarily as a consequence of the prior gratification of the more demanding animal needs, we should certainly speak less exclusively of self-control…and more frequently of self-choice.… To be impulse-aware, to know that we really want and need love, respect, knowledge, a philosophy, self-actualization…this is a difficult psychological achievement… Not only is it good to survive, but it is also good for the person to grow toward full humanness, toward actualization of his potentialities, toward…peak experiences, toward transcendence, toward richer and more accurate cognition to reality. No longer need we rest on sheer viability and survival as our only ultimate proof that poverty or war or domination or cruelty are bad, rather than good. We can consider them bad because they also degrade the quality of life, of personality, of consciousness, of wisdom."[22]

CURIOSITY

*Above and beyond these negative determinants for acquiring knowledge…there are some reasonable grounds for postulating positive per se impulses to **satisfy curiosity**, to know, to explain, and to understand.*

– ABRAHAM MASLOW

Kids take risks because they are innately inquisitive and curious, and they play. As adults, we seemingly have forgotten how to play. With knowledge, bolstered by perspective and agency, we are able to hold paradox and aspire to something much greater than our individuality. Our curiosity is reinvigorated and reminds us that, as poet and essayist Diane Ackerman states, "It's our passion for deep play that makes us the puzzling and at times resplendent beings we are."[23]

I'll further defer to the wizarding words of Elizabeth Gilbert on curiosity:

> "…curiosity only ever asks one simple question: 'Is there anything you're interested in?'…it's a clue… Following that scavenger hunt of curiosity can lead you to amazing, unexpected places. It may even eventually lead you to your passion—albeit through a strange, untraceable passageway of back alleys, underground caves, and secret doors. Or it may lead you nowhere. You might spend your whole life following your curiosity and have absolutely nothing to show for it at the end—except one thing. You will have the satisfaction of knowing that you passed

your entire existence in devotion to the noble human virtue of inquisitiveness."[24]

Curiosity is about readiness to make our own hero's journey. It asks us to suspend judgment—holding off on indulging, distracting, or denying—and just be with the experience at hand, in its entirety.

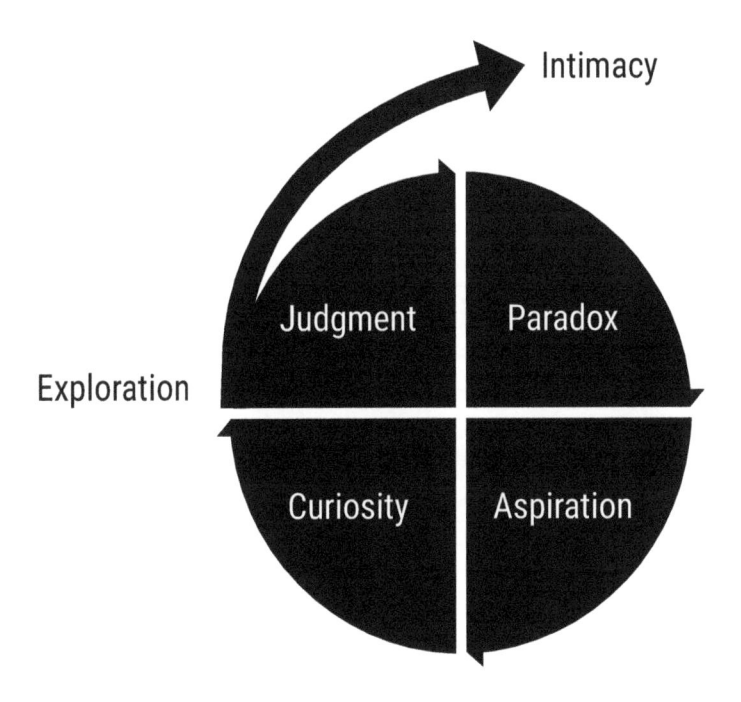

Intimacy

Exploration

Judgment | *Paradox*
Curiosity | *Aspiration*

In the satisfaction of curiosity, we are able to tolerate taking risk. Reengaging with our imaginations and "playing" with the possibilities allows us to explore the unknown, and as Carl Jung is summarized: "We have to act, that is, respond to the demands of the unconscious by tending to our dreams, doing active imagination, reflecting on synchronicities we notice in daily life, and working with any fantasies that arise.

Because the unconscious generally acts in compensatory ways to our conscious orientation, these products of our inner life often clash with the ego mind. The result is that we experience…the 'tension of opposites,' and to encourage the development of the transcendent function, we need to *hold* this tension. Holding the tension of opposites is not pleasant or easy, so we suffer."[25]

By embracing our paradoxical natures, our perspective shifts from ordinary to extraordinary, and we are readied to heed the great call of our lives.

Transformed by paradox arising to meet aspiration, judgment gives way to curiosity. From the satisfied need for exploration emerges the need for intimacy, and our developmental trajectory shifts from independence to interdependence.

Being Needs and the Sufferings of Spirit

One does not complain about water because it is wet, or about rocks because they are hard, or about trees because they are green. As the child looks out upon the world with wide, uncritical, undemanding, innocent eyes, simply noting and observing what is the case, without either arguing the matter or demanding that it be otherwise, so does the self-actualizing person tend to look upon human nature in himself and in others.

—ABRAHAM MASLOW, *MOTIVATION AND PERSONALITY*

Maslow's hierarchy, when depicted in its iconic pyramid, portrays development as a linear model of acquisition and achievement with the promise of all things, should you reach its tip. Fostered by the hidden messages of our American societal norms—win at all costs and do it alone—the pyramid falsely communicates that once you figure out the first level, you reap its rewards, move to the next, and so on, until you reach the zenith. This couldn't be further from the truth of Maslow's theory.[1]

Development is anything but linear, and it is definitely not something to be achieved. While being human equips us with a vast developmental toolbox, access to and dexterity with its tools is not necessarily assured. Suffering calls us to seek this assurance.

While the needs plot the common human developmental trajectory of dependence, independence, interdependence, and transcendence, events occur across our lifetimes, creating a unique road for each one of us to travel. Events of love and harm, initiation and transition, loss and grief, as well as those of defeat and accomplishment call us with unique songs of suffering. Each song implores us to choose, to transform, to dissolve our previous self, and to create a new self with new abilities and circumstances.

Every event is distinctly experienced, challenging and rechallenging our tolerance to need frustration. Forever cycling through experiential creation, transformation, and dissolution, we can spin aimlessly with the competing demands of each of the needs, but suffering gives us direction. Suffering points us to our most unmet, prepotent need and the places we must travel to satisfy it, regardless of our maturity in the trajectory of development. Defying the notion of linearity, suffering takes one step forward, two steps back.

The basic needs and the sufferings of survival help to shape our orientation to the external world. The becoming needs and the sufferings of self serve to educate us about our internal world—the sense of self and its structure, as well as the mind and the depth of its possibilities. The being needs and the sufferings of spirit reveal to us the interconnected and creative essence present within each one of us.

Reflective of the bridge that the becoming needs serve— reaching from the physical, external world through the mental, internal world to the mystical, universal world— current research has updated Maslow's characteristics of self-actualized humans. "Maslow asserted that 'self-actualizing individuals are able to paradoxically merge with a common humanity while at the same time able to maintain a strong identity and sense of self.'"[2] Operating under this truth, the investigation applied Maslow's hierarchy to modern life and demonstrated the key to understanding this intertwining of development, needs, experience and suffering. When its operational code shifts from one of deficiency and stability to one of growth and plasticity, the human system is optimized.[3]

In accordance with the science of self-actualized characteristics, the transformative developmental tasks— practicing prediction, invoking the pause, gaining perspective, holding paradox, committing to persevere, playing with passion—and their paired faculties of development— attention, attachment, agency, aspiration, acceptance, and awareness—are the tools crucial to satisfying our human needs, reimagining and understanding the necessity of suffering, and shifting our operational code:

- Efficient perception of reality: The sufferings of survival narrow our reality to seek safety and connection, signatures of the dependent stage of development. Satisfied in the basic

needs, becoming needs emerge. The need for esteem and its suffering of ignorance, when transformed by gaining a broader perception and acting with agency, gives rise to the knowledge needed to explore the truth of reality.
- Continued freshness of appreciation: Independence fully unfolds with the need for exploration and its suffering of judgment, when transformed by holding paradox and living with aspiration, curiosity appears. As curiosity further blossoms, appreciation, wonder, awe, and gratitude are routine to daily life.
- Equanimity: From curiosity, the need for intimacy emerges. The suffering of isolation ushers in the developmental task of perseverance where equanimity allows us to fully experience the vacillations of life without being carried away by them.
- Acceptance: The need for intimacy and its suffering of isolation, mitigated by perseverance, gives rise to acceptance, first of one's self so we then may be of service and in acceptance of others.
- Good moral intuition: Internalizing the knowledge previously gained and aspirational living opens us to the ethical guidance of the universal senses of imagination, insight, and intuition.
- Humanitarianism: Acceptance and the developmental call of interdependence combine in the satisfaction of compassion, and prosocial interests are asserted.
- Purpose: Satisfied in compassion, we are called toward the great task of our life. The highest of needs, purpose, is transformed in the suffering of longing. Playing with passion bolstered by the other, more prepotent developmental tasks, reveals the faculty of awareness.

- Creative spirit: As awareness stabilizes, our perspective further shifts. Creativity draws us further into wisdom.
- Peak experiences: Creativity and wisdom work through us, opening us to actualization and transcendence.[4]

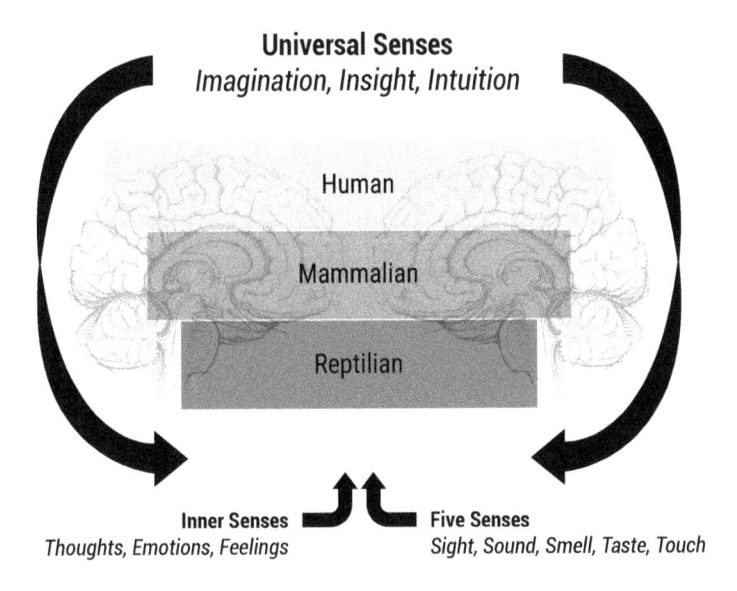

Universal Senses
Imagination, Insight, Intuition

Human

Mammalian

Reptilian

Inner Senses
Thoughts, Emotions, Feelings

Five Senses
Sight, Sound, Smell, Taste, Touch

Modern day has asked us to turn away not only from our creatureliness but also the sacredness found in our existence. Confusion of spirituality with religion, mostly as interchangeable experiences, has severely impacted our willingness to engage with uncertainty and the unknown. We must constantly manage the tension between the prepotent, gravitational pull of deficiency in the material and the evolutionary push toward growth in the mystery. Spirituality, regardless of how it otherwise is exercised in a religious or secular manner, is absolutely necessary for a fully actualized life.

Returning once again to researcher and storyteller Brené Brown: "Spirituality is recognizing and celebrating that we are all inextricably connected to each other by a power greater than all of us, and that our connection to that power and to one another is grounded in love and compassion. Practicing spirituality brings a sense of perspective, meaning, and purpose to our lives"[5]

Much of our lives are focused on fussing about the contents of the body-mind—its sensations, feelings, emotions, thoughts, images. Unfortunately, this fussing precludes many of us from ever inquiring into the context by which it all happens. This context is consciousness, the "power greater than all of us."

The being needs and sufferings of spirit, isolation and longing, invite us to surrender to this latent power. They ask us to be conscious of consciousness, open to the mystery, to the deepest part of who we really are. Jack Kornfield, in *The Wise Heart*, further frames this invitation:

> "It is an urgent task for the psychology of our time to understand and foster the highest possibilities of human development. The suffering and happiness in our world, both individual and collective, depend on our consciousness. We have to find a wiser way to live."[6]

Isolation.

Suffering is the catalyst that calls you into a state of reflection or action. If you lived a life without suffering, you would never learn, mature, or strengthen yourself. You would never find the impetus in a carefree existence to look within and find out who you truly are and develop your character.
—ST. JOHN OF THE CROSS, *THE DARK NIGHT OF THE SOUL*

In the sterile hospital room, light poured from the dingy window falling on a couple deep in love—fully present in this time, in this place. He, younger, well-kempt but obviously falling to pieces. She, bedridden and gaunt yet glowing with the insight of knowing one's own mortality. Their eyes were locked, not a word was spoken nor needed to be. The intimacy was so solid it prevented me from moving farther into the space of the room. With my weight supported by the door frame, I watched in absolute wonder.

With a quick intake of breath followed by a sharp groan, the pain of cancer broke the spell. Gently laying a hand upon her chest, he leaned in with helplessness and fear. The pain subsided, allowing them to finally recognize my presence. A white coat and stethoscope signal my role. Strangely, I feel compelled to acknowledge their shared intimacy and the beauty of it, perhaps a wish to further delay the discussion of the elephant in the room.

They tell the story of their May-to-December romance that spans two decades. Both academics, they are merged in both body and mind. Gazing into each other's eyes, their story flows, and I am once again enveloped into the cocoon of the intimacy present when I first entered the room. Abruptly, she turns her gaze away from her beloved, and with eyes blazing, she turns toward me. Imbued with layer upon layer of emotion and deep curiosity, she asks, "My whole life, I have treated my body as a temple. Why does it fail me now? Please tell me, good doctor, why does my body fail me *now*?"

Death is our great teacher of intimacy. I think this is why we abhor it so much. Death magnifies the very power of intimate relationships, and it scares us. It also unleashes the paradox of intimacy—something we all wish for and deeply desire but fear we may never have or the risk of losing it is altogether too great—leaving us too vulnerable to even try. Consider any story where profound heartache from loss and the resulting tidal waves of grief crash into the shores of meaninglessness. This illustrates, as author Angeles Arrien puts it, that "life's greatest remorse is love unexpressed"—remorse in the unexpressed love for others and the exquisite tenderness of the unexpressed self-love known deep within our spirits.[1]

Erik Erikson, celebrated psychoanalyst best known for his theory on the life cycle, recognized the relationship between intimacy and isolation. He described intimacy as "the ability to fuse your identity with somebody else's, without fear that you are going to lose something yourself…to be intimate, you have to have a firm identity already."[2] Erikson's theory also emphasizes what he terms *crises,* "turning points or crucial moments" in human development. In the stage of intimacy, isolation is the crisis. Erikson states: "Such crises… do not only decide possible individual maldevelopment but—more important in this context—what…may lead to the establishment of what I call a forbidding inner shell, which prevents people from being aware of their potentials…" Despite its framing in a continuum of chronological age development, one could argue Erikson's crises ring with the sufferings of unmet needs.[3]

All suffering has an inherent element of separation, as its envelopment of the sufferer creates a bubble of disconnection with others and the world at large. The suffering of isolation is the dark night of the soul, the deepest of separations we can experience as a human. It is a time in life when we are asked to revisit all unprocessed sufferings, bring them forward, and accept what Carl Jung posited when he said, "There is only one thing that seems to work, and that is to turn directly toward the approaching darkness without prejudice and totally naively, and to try to find out what its secret aim is and what it wants from you."[4]

In his tribute to Jung, philosopher Alan Watts identifies that the suffering of isolation is required for the integration of our own "element of malice…of irreducible rascality." Watts further contextualizes this suffering as "not as something to be condemned and wailed over, but as something to be recognized as contributive to one's greatness and to one's positive aspects, in the same way that manure is contributive to the perfume of the rose."[5]

St. John of the Cross, author of the *Dark Night of the Soul*, describes the suffering of isolation as first beginning with a reorienting away from the material world. Senses, desires, worldly attachments become much less interesting. Stripped of desire and identity, the suffering of isolation can be suffocating while living in our very materialistic world. Enduring overshadows enjoyment, and our curiosity unveils the true work of our lives, where the dark night then calls us to question the ephemeral nature of our strongest emotions, the meaning of our most cherished memories, and the pain of our deepest wounds. Through this solitary experience of transformation, we open to fully accept ourselves. Only through the acceptance of ourselves can we accept the fullness of others and the world at large, giving birth to a life of joy, service, interdependent love, and compassion.[6]

INTIMACY: DO I FULLY ACCEPT MYSELF?

Owning our story can be hard but not nearly as difficult as spending our life running from it. Embracing our vulnerabilities is risky but not nearly as dangerous as giving up on love and belonging and joy—the experiences that make us the most vulnerable. Only when we can be brave enough to explore the darkness will we discover the infinite power of our light.

— BRENÉ BROWN, *THE GIFTS OF IMPERFECTION*

Experientially, I have come to understand that many people function in a developmental range of codependence to fierce independence, living lives enmeshed or in parallel with those around them. On occasion, I have cared for highly developed individuals whose lives were infused with love and compassion. Both secular and religious, these highly spiritual patients understood that we are all interconnected and responsible to care for one another and our communities. Interdependent by nature, they intentionally live lives of service and deep faith. Sadly, the suffering of isolation pervades this group of individuals as they grapple with doubt and struggle with the intimacy of sharing their pain and receiving the love they so often offer from their own stance of service.

Serving as precursors to self-actualization, we need all the prepotent dimensions of curiosity to satisfy our need for intimacy:

- *Joyous Exploration* is based on Edward Deci's work (see Self-Determination Theory we discussed earlier), and this aspect of curiosity reflects the French notion of "joie de vivre." Quoting the team who did the research on curiosity, joyous exploration is "being consumed with wonder about the fascinating features of the world."
- *Deprivation Sensitivity* is an odd part of curiosity in that it enables us to see a hole in our situation, driving us to solve a problem or fill in the knowledge gap.
- *Social Curiosity*, unsurprisingly, calls to our inherent social nature to understand other creatures. We need to observe and engage with others to learn about them.
- *Stress Tolerance* is the choice we make to persevere. It is the ability to accept the entirety of the "terrible sublime."
- *Thrill Seeking* is about taking risk. It takes stress tolerance and amplifies the energy toward experiencing something new, especially if it is intense.[7]

Curiosity prepares us for the dark night of the soul. This force takes us across the dubious threshold of *The Hero's Journey*. In making the choice to cross the threshold, we choose to "live a life that is more strongly driven by curiosity than by fear." Further quoting Elizabeth Gilbert, "we all know that fear is a desolate boneyard where our dreams go to desiccate in the hot sun…fear is boring…fear is a deeply ancient instinct…and an evolutionarily vital one.…but it ain't especially smart…fear [is unoriginal]."[8]

Have you ever wondered what it feels like to experience you? Think of someone you adore. What is the experience of them… what are the sensations, feelings, emotions, moods, insights their presence brings to you? Invoking your curiosity, now flip that around. The suffering of isolation begs us to answer the question: *Do I fully accept myself?* Understanding that to be of service and to love others wholeheartedly, I must first love myself.

Although the suffering of isolation requires us to turn inward, we need the reciprocal support of another or a small network of others who serve as a "mirror, reflecting who we are and who we are not."[9] One of the more beautiful things of the twenty-first century is our redefinition of intimate relationships. Following the diaspora of the family in the post–World War II boom of higher education and the social revolution of the 1960s, our traditional ideas of intimacy have been challenged.[10] The myth that one person should be your best friend, lover, and go-to for all things safety is finally being debunked, unburdening the spousal relationship from undue responsibility. Calling for a network of intimate, friend, and communal connections, the Surgeon General, Dr. Vivek Murthy, reflects this shifting dynamic of relational life:

> "A close confidante or intimate partner—someone with whom you share a deep mutual bond of affection and trust...quality friendships and social companionship and support...a network or community of people who share your sense of purpose and interests. These three dimensions together reflect the full range of high-quality social connections that humans need in order to thrive. The lack of relationships in any of these dimensions can make us lonely, which helps to explain why we may have a supportive marriage yet still feel lonely for friends and community."[11]

These relationships of interdependence reflect what Maslow called "being love," recognizing the difference in more intimate, meaningful relational experiences relative to those of "deficiency love" found in meeting the basic need for connection. Interestingly, many other psychologists and contemplative practitioners have also found ways to articulate this difference. Said by Scott Barry Kaufman: "Personal salvation and what is good for the person alone cannot be really understood in isolation... the good of other people must be invoked, as well as the good for oneself..."[12]

Similarly stated, both Erich Fromm and Irvin Yalom, esteemed humanistic scholars in their own rights, believe love is "an attitude." Fromm goes on to say that "love is active, not a passive process; an attitude, not a feeling." Kaufman builds further on Maslow and Fromm to state that, "as a person matures, and the needs of others become just as important as the needs of one's self, a person gradually transforms the idea of love from 'being loved' into 'loving.'"[13]

Beth and Laird, the intimate couple from the story above, leaned into Beth's cancer and her perceived defiance of her body. Together they peered into its murkiness, and anger emerged. Anger was not a familiar emotion for Beth, yet its fierceness seemed to be pointing her toward something. With the loving stability of Laird's presence, Beth embraced her anger. A young part of her felt jilted in the contract she had made with the God of her youth. Beth felt this part of her in her chest, the primary source of her pain and from which scorching diatribes and condemnations poured forth, in what Beth described as a river of molten lava. Reliving all the "shoulds" of her younger years, Beth felt the fear and shame this part of her had been carrying for decades. Supported by their neighbor and good friend, Jon, and Beth's sister Ester, Laird held her and listened, reassuring Beth of the wise, mature version of herself in the present.

Given its long-sought attention, this part of Beth eased its hold, and Beth was breathless and exhausted, yet seemingly revitalized. She had found a deep well of gratitude, its cool waters able to soothe the intensity of the lava. With the pain and anger transformed, Beth and Laird had several days of lucidly rich conversation and togetherness before she was discharged home. Two months later, Laird phoned to let me know that Beth had died. Laird's voice had taken a tone of powerful self-assuredness that had not been present previously. He relayed that somehow in those last days Beth had imbued him with strength to endure her death, and though he will forever carry the weight of his grief, he was assured that he could.

Beth and Laird's story reminds me of a saying often credited to legendary Chinese philosopher Lao Tzu, "Being deeply loved by someone gives you strength while loving someone deeply gives you courage…" Armed with curiosity, strength, and courage, we are able to cross the threshold.

COMMITTING TO PERSEVERE

In each moment we have a choice: we can perpetuate our suffering, or we can interrupt that pattern at its source and attain a glimpse of liberation.
— CHÖGYAM TRUNGPA, THE TRUTH OF SUFFERING

Perseverance is exercised in our gifted ability to choose. As powerfully said by Viktor Frankl, "between stimulus and response there is a space. In that space is our power to choose our response. In our response lies our growth and our freedom."[14] In filling that space with perseverance, all our needs, faculties, and skills combine in the personally perfected recipe for the delights of acceptance and compassion, particularly self-compassion.

Having stepped across the threshold into the dark night of the soul, we enter into a process that is known across all humanity. As introduced in the suffering of judgment, *The Hero's Journey* is the great monomyth that the contemplative writer Joseph Campbell dedicated his life to exploring. As Campbell's work displays, heroes exist across all cultures, creeds, and communities.[15] The scientific tradition is no exception, as *The Hero's Journey* is also mirrored in the shared human experience of dying.

In the 1960s, we saw the birth of resuscitation science, the practices and procedures involving bringing life back to those whose hearts have stopped beating or lungs have stopped breathing. While contributing to the explosion of medical knowledge that began in the years following World War II, resuscitation or, as most of you know it, CPR, has also given us a new population of people to study—those with near-death experiences. In 1975, Dr. Raymond Moody, who holds doctorates in both medicine and philosophy, published *Life after Life*. A phenomenological report of near-death experiences written for the public, *Life after Life* still remains a global best seller.[16] Although Moody's work has been picked up by many, Dr. Sam Parnia, an active researcher and intensivist, is demonstrating significant expansion of Moody's work in exploring the far reaches of consciousness, especially the evidence of its existence after death.

Parnia has renamed near-death experiences to *recalled experiences of death (RED),* due to the growing number of reported transcendent experiences because of meditation, the use of psychedelics, and outcomes of somatic psychotherapies.[17] It seems the experiences related to being declared "dead" and returning to life were being lost in the fray. First described in the *Annals of The New York Academy of Sciences* in 2022 and further detailed in his 2024 book, *Lucid Dying,* Parnia lays out the four-stage narrative arc of dying described by those who have been called to return:

> Consciousness senses a separation of selfhood from the body, preparing for the journey→
>
> Anticipatory planning for the journey→
>
> Journey unfolds through a meaningful life review→
>
> Journey culminates with the sense of "being" home

He describes the process as an "internal transcendent, hyperconscious, lucid experience" that gradually moves us from the waking world into the "grey zone of death." Lockstep with the key components to *The Hero's Journey* of heeding the call, crossing the threshold, undergoing the transformational ordeal, and the return, REDs map out the process of perseverance that dying can teach us about living.[18]

Dying is *the* living mythology. When our development shifts with the emergence of the becoming needs, the suffering of judgment calls us to our journey. The suffering of isolation asks us to heed the call, and the journey begins. Through perseverance, we undergo the meaningful life review, the ordeal of the dark night of the soul. Using the myth of death, we have an age-old process to lean on for guidance and direction to commit to living a fully actualized life.

Parnia describes the life review as a minutely detailed procession where we "simultaneously experience thousands of memories and images, whilst also fully experiencing them individually and independently." Key insights gained in the review involve "understanding the 'cause and effect' of relationships—*the chain of reasons*—behind all the events in [our] lives, together with the longer-term downstream consequences—*the domino cascade*—of [our] own and other people's actions."[19]

At the bedside of a Native American woman, I was told a tale shared in her tradition about the process of life review. Her people believed that throughout our lifetime, we leave shards of our spirit throughout our pasts. Shards are the discarded younger parts of ourselves that were overwhelmed by the experience of life. The tale goes on to instruct that during life, when our maturity allows, we must retrieve those shards of our spirit, bringing them into the present, to once again make the spirit whole. Those shards that remain at the end of our lives will be collected through the process of death and dying. She was clear there was a reason they used the word shard—shards are sharp, misshapen, difficult to handle, and can cut like a blade. They hurt. She was also crystal clear on the tale's lesson: It is important to do this work in life, to persevere; otherwise, all the hurt comes in death.

A powerful tale for the toughest task we have as humans, and I was bowled over in its telling. Collecting shards has become the metaphor for my daily work—with myself and with others. Shards work can be found across many traditions—shaman soul retrieval is usually the first to come to most people's minds. In science, we have parts therapy.

In a beautiful marriage of lessons, dying can teach us about living, parts therapy (IFS) provides a practical process for collecting our shards. As previously discussed, we have Exiles, Managers, and Firefighters that have been left across our past. Using the work you have already done through the deathbed exercise, the map of your life is drafted, and the compass of suffering is readily available to guide you in the retrieval of your own life's shards.

ACCEPTANCE
This being human is a guest house.
Every morning a new arrival.

A joy, a depression, a meanness,
some momentary awareness comes
as an unexpected visitor.

Welcome and entertain them all!
Even if they are a crowd of sorrows,
who violently sweep your house
empty of its furniture,
still, treat each guest honorably.
He may be clearing you out
for some new delight.

The dark thought, the shame, the malice,
meet them at the door laughing,
and invite them in.

Be grateful for whoever comes,
because each has been sent
as a guide from beyond.

— RUMI, *THE GUEST HOUSE*

I recently stumbled across a profound discussion of lived acceptance. Broadcast journalist Anderson Cooper interviewed late-night television personality Stephen Colbert on his podcast, *All There Is*. Together they discussed the pain of loss, the experience of grief, and their shared suffering. Colbert is the youngest of eleven children, and when he was ten, his two older brothers and his father were killed in an accident. He was the only remaining child at home with his widowed mother.

This wise man was talking to a very aggrieved Anderson Cooper, who had just lost his mother, Gloria Vanderbilt. Cooper was struggling with the realization that he was the last remaining member of his family of origin. His father died of heart disease when Cooper was ten and his brother died by suicide during Cooper's twenties. It was astonishing to me to be able to see these men sit so vulnerably and talk about this profound human experience of suffering and how it touched them:

> AC: You told an interviewer that you have learned to, in your words, "love the thing that I most wish had not happened." You went on to say, "What punishments of God are not gifts?" Do you really believe that?

> SC: Yes. It's a gift to exist. And with existence comes suffering. There's no escaping that… But if you are grateful for your life…then you have to be grateful for all of it…

> And so, at a young age, I suffered something. So that by the time I was in serious relationships in my life—with friends or with my wife or with my children—I have some understanding that everybody

is suffering. And however imperfectly, to acknowledge their suffering and connect with them and to love them in a deep way…makes you grateful for the fact that you have suffered so that you can know that about other people…

I want to be the most human I can be, and that involves acknowledging and ultimately being grateful for the things that I wish didn't happen, because they gave me a gift…

AC: I've thought about that endlessly…in order to be fully human, you have to, you have to go through this suffering. You have to, suffering is a part of existence.

SC: And acceptance of that suffering is not defeat.

AC: What do you mean?

SC: We think we can win against grief. We think we can fix it. But you can't. You can only experience it…grief is not a bad thing. Grief is a reaction to a bad thing. Grief itself is a natural process that has to be experienced… But in fact, addressing your grief and sharing your grief and telling that story and you telling me about your brother and me telling you about my brothers, actually opens us up to other feelings and other possibilities…in fact, grief is a doorway to another you.[20]

The key here is the exemplified opening to other feelings and possibilities that Colbert so eloquently shared.

Acceptance is not defeat. Built on attention, attachment, agency, and aspiration, acceptance is a simple recognition of a powerful event and its impact on your life. Acceptance is recognizing a part of you is suffering an unmet need as a result. Though simple, it is far from easy. Acceptance is using suffering as a compass, pointing you toward wholeness, should you so choose.

Revisiting our life's most tender spots is no work for the faint of heart, but it is clearly essential to fully living. In the words of Jungian psychologist James Hillman, "Our theories favor traumas setting us the task of working them through. Despite early injury and all the slings and arrows of outrageous fortune, we bear from the start the image of a definite individual character with some enduring traits. So this [journey] wants to repair some of that damage by showing what else was there, is there, in your nature. It wants to resurrect the unaccountable twists that turned your boat around in the eddies and shallows of meaninglessness, bringing you back to feelings of destiny. For that is what is lost in so many lives, and what must be recovered: a sense of personal calling, that there is a reason I am alive."[21]

The practice of shard retrieval requires that you find time and space to fully attend to the present moment. As noted previously, there is nothing like the approach of death to call one's attention. This is one of its lessons. Attend to your life, just like you would your death. So, find a quiet space with dedicated time to further explore your deathbed scene and its five most salient words.

Ideally, you'd have several uninterrupted hours where you have no other responsibilities. You will need time to prepare your space, go through the exercise, and then rest and digest after its completion. Let's begin:

> Working from our previous exercise, have your five most salient words at hand. You may also want to have a box of tissues, as the process can be emotional. Additionally, you may need pen and paper to capture your experience.
>
> First settle your body into a comfortable position where you can allow it to remain still for a period of time. Remaining mentally alert, close your eyes. Attend to the breath. Just watch it come and go in its own natural rhythm.
>
> As sensory experiences arise, allow them to flow freely. If you find yourself attaching to any thought, feeling, emotion, or sensation, notice that and make a choice…let go and return to the breath, or choose to refocus your attention to what you've attached to. Remain purposefully attached to your object of attention—breath or sensation—just watching, letting it flow through you. Be careful to remain unengaged in the object, just letting them flow in their own natural rhythm.
>
> The body-mind will continue to sequentially process information, as that is its evolutionary function. Act with agency to allow this natural flow of information

to run through your system. Continue to breathe, returning to your object of attention when you find your mind has let go of its hold.

After a few breaths, and when your mind is settled enough, pick up your five most salient words. Beginning with the fifth word listed, say the word silently several times. Reclose your eyes if they aren't already. Continue to silently repeat the word. When you hear this word internally, where do you feel it in your body? What are the qualities? Are there sensations? Feelings or emotions? Thoughts or images? There may be nothing. Just inquire and aspire to bring this word alive in your life. Stay here as long as you like. You may want to journal to further process origin and meaning of this aspiration. Feel free to do so, if you wish.

When ready, resettle into your reflective position. Breathing, attending. Return to your list and identify the fourth word. Begin silently and gently repeating the word, allowing it to be your object of attention. Note where in the body the word most resonates. What sensations, feelings, thoughts, and emotions arise when you attend to this word in your body? Any memories? Any desires? Inquire and aspire. How does this aspiration shape your life? Linger as long as you wish; journal as necessary.

Difficult experiences may arise. As they do, know that you are safe and secure in the present. Allow the past to come forward, as much as you wish. With each sensation or emotion, thought or feeling, spend time with it. Is one experience calling your attention most? Focus there. Breathe. Does the part of you have an age? A name? What is its important story? Breathe. Give your full attention to this part of you; accept its suffering as a simple call to its most unmet need.

You may feel other parts arise with emotions, sensations, feelings, and thoughts. Breathe and remember you are safe in the present. Ask any protective parts if it would be okay to listen to the story together. If the protectors aren't quite ready, turn your attention there—reassuring safety in the present, inquiring into their stories, accepting and aspiring to be with them fully.

With permission and when you are ready, together return to the original part's story. As it unfolds, reassure the part and its protectors that you are safe and in the present. Continue listening. When the part's story is finished, ask if the part is ready to return its shard and come with you into the present. What role does it wish to play now that it is free of its history? Again, attend and inquire, accept. To what does this part aspire?

Journal when you feel the need. There is no right or wrong; just freely jot down what comes to mind. It may be words or pictures; all are welcome. Perhaps note the details of your parts and their shards—where they are located in your body, their ages, preferences, their sufferings. No need to think, just allow it to come to the paper. Pause here if you wish or need to continue journaling.

When ready, resettle into your reflective position. Breathing, attending. Return to your list and identify the third word. Gently repeat the word internally, allowing it to be your object of attention. Where does your body register the word? If any, what sensations, feelings, thoughts, and emotions are present? Any attachments, desires, or wants? Any specific memory arising? Inquire and aspire. What does this word mean to you?

Stay here, addressing any parts that may come up. Attend, accept, aspire, and know you have agency in the present moment. Reassure the part you are safe in the present, inquire about it, attend to its story and the shard it holds. If protectors arise, reassure them too, inquire into their attachments, attend and, with permission, together return to the original part. Breathe, attend, inquire, accept, aspire. If you feel journaling will help, feel free to do so.

Breathe.

Drawing your attention to the present moment, resettle, close your eyes. Recall the second word on your list. Whispering it repeatedly with your internal voice, allow it to settle in your body. Where do you feel it, sense it? What are the qualities? Any parts arising? Attend, inquire, accept, aspire.

Breathe. Write, draw, if you wish.

Again, returning to the scene of your deathbed, recall the topmost word on your list. Internalize the word; repeat it softly. To what does it aspire? Does it have feelings, emotions, sensations? Thoughts or images? Are there parts or their protectors that require your attention? Stay to inquire to their attachments, their sufferings. Accept. Aspire.

Journal, draw, doodle. Breathe.

Widening your attention to the entirety of your body-mind, note how the stories of the five salient words are woven together throughout your body. How are they related to each other? Spend time attending and inquiring into the connection points between the words. Work through sensations, feelings, emotions, thoughts, and memories as they arise. Attend to parts and protectors, accepting their stories, their sufferings. Aspire to embody their stories. What shards remain? Aspire to embody the five words.

Remain here as long as you need. Breathe, journal, draw.

When you are ready, take a few deep breaths and slowly open your eyes. Wiggle fingers and toes. Stretch the body. Taking a slow walk or soaking in a bath may further help to incorporate your gathered shards. Wrapped in the aspirations of your life, rest.

Once you have rested and processed, I would encourage you to share this with a trusted person. Share the premise of IFS, the shard practice, and your five most salient words. Ask them to listen with an open mind, describe your findings of the practice. Can they help you understand specific details? Share with them how their personhood is experienced in your life, especially in the manifestation of the five salient words. Express your gratitude to this person and how you wish your relationship to continue to evolve.

COMPASSION

The fruit of transcending our small self is the awakening of reverence, a newfound spirit of compassion and holy interdependence...the power of a concentrated mind can be directed toward the creation of suffering or well-being.
— JACK KORNFIELD, *THE WISE HEART*

Compassion, the ability to be with someone else in their experience, is a self-generating energy for all parties involved, as the holder receives the energy in the form of contemplative service, and the one being held receives the energy of being held, of feeling felt. Typically, we associate compassion as being with someone in their suffering, but arguably, since the Germans have a word for it, freudenfreude, compassion can also mean to be with someone in their joy and well-being.[22]

Scott Berry Kaufman offers a beautiful description of what it means to be satisfied in the need for intimacy and the ability to extend compassion and its components to others:

> "Whenever you are in the presence of [someone satisfied in intimacy], you can't help but feel uplifted.

She seems to bring out the best in everyone, due in large part to her own ability to spot the best in others. Everyone wants [her] on their team, not only because of her abundance of love but also because she is extremely thoughtful and dependable. While [she] emits so much light, she doesn't sacrifice her own needs and is able to take care of herself when she must, and she speaks her mind in a way that makes others want to listen to her viewpoint. [She] tends to see the greater humanity in nearly every situation and discussion and tries her best to see some merit in all the different perspectives on the table."[23]

Feeling compassion is necessary to truly experience safety and connection. Safety and connection allow us to feel vulnerable. In that vulnerability, we open to curiosity and growth. Growth happens when we accept ourselves fully, and from it compassion surfaces. At first, it is self-compassion. Self-compassion then can be paid forward by extending it to others, thus creating the self-generative energy compassion brings to the world.

According to Dr. Kristin Neff, psychological researcher, compassion—of self and others—has three components: ability to see or be mindful of the present moment and its sufferings, kindness as opposed to judgment, and a perspective of shared common humanity as opposed to isolation.[24] The need for intimacy reflects the human condition of deep interconnectedness, the shared common humanity of Neff's definition, and as neuroscientist John Cacioppo clearly articulates, "our neural, hormonal, and genetic makeup support interdependence over independence."[25]

According to Cornell professor of psychology Dr. Robert Sternberg, interdependent relationships require the triangular interplay of intimacy, passion, and commitment. He also cleverly discusses the geometry of the "love triangle" as determined by the "amount" and "balance" of each component, with the example of an equilateral triangle representing "complete love," the full combination of all three components. Sternberg also invokes the collective power of stories to better conceptualize people's experiences and understanding of love. Ranging from "War. Love is a series of battles in a devastating but continuing war" to "Sewing. Love is whatever you make it," the stories we tell about love and compassion can help us determine the degree to which we are suffering or satisfied in our need for intimacy.[26] Intimacy requires your full presence, your full commitment, as it is the flow of relationship with compassion as its source.

When the energy of compassion repeatedly calls us to people and circumstances best suited to continually meet our needs, our relationship to work and others provides a mutuality full of vitality and buoyancy. This shift toward compassionate perspective provides a wellspring of equanimity, joy, and loving-kindness described in Kaufman's above ideal and sets the grounding for mutual trust, reciprocity, and respect. From this grounding, we can forgive those who have harmed us, seek forgiveness from those whom we have harmed and, most important, we can forgive ourselves. Reparations, reconciliation, and renewal are made possible.

To this end, intimacy, compassion, and interconnection underpin the greatest of human powers—cooperation. Our evolutionary power of cooperation is rooted in our shared human imagination, as historian Yuval Noah Harari elucidates in his groundbreaking work *Sapiens*, first articulated in his 2015 TED Talk:

> "The only animal that can combine the two abilities together and cooperate both flexibly and still do so in very large numbers is us, Homo sapiens… What enables us alone, of all the animals, to cooperate in such a way? The answer is our imagination…over the centuries, we have constructed on top of this objective reality a second layer of fictional reality, a reality made of fictional entities like nations, like gods, like money, like corporations…this fictional reality became more and more powerful so that today, the most powerful forces in the world are these fictional entities. Today, the very survival of rivers and trees and lions and elephants depends on the decisions and wishes of fictional entities, like the United States, like Google, like the World Bank—entities that exist only in our own imagination."[27]

Through the act of acceptance, we foster self-compassion. From self-compassion, we are able to be compassionate with others. When we are compassionate with others, its generative energy allows for cooperation, the inspiration to imagine, and the open possibility to create our shared reality.

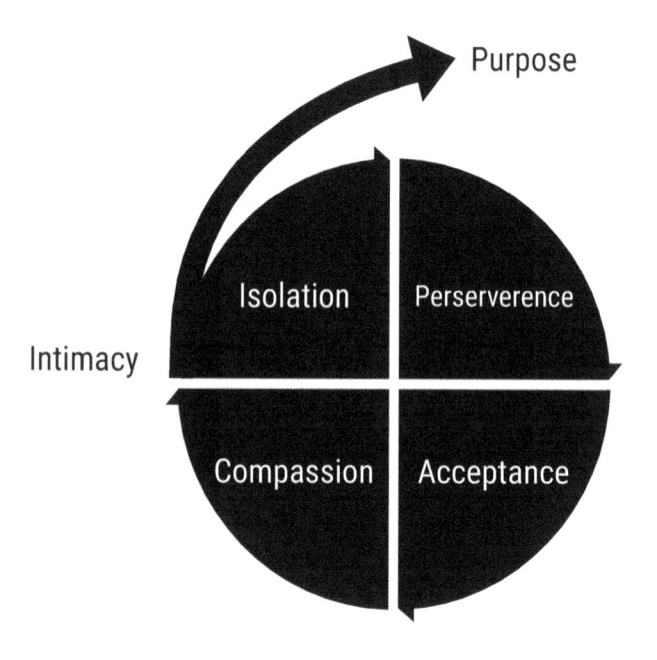

```
                    Purpose
          ↗
   ┌─────────┬─────────┐
   │ Isolation│Perserverence│
Intimacy    │         │
   ├─────────┼─────────┤
   │Compassion│Acceptance│
   └─────────┴─────────┘
```

From inspiration and the satisfaction of compassion, we begin to receive insights and intuition to something greater, sparks of actualization occur, and the suffering of longing emerges.

The developmental function of transcendence begins. The conscious has integrated with unconscious, further strengthening the self with curiosity and finally tempering it with acceptance. When you gain the direct knowledge of the self, the ability to shift the sensory input from outward reaching to inward receiving reveals a new perspective called awareness, the being part of existence.

Longing.

One should not search for an abstract meaning of life. Everyone has his own specific vocation or mission in life to carry out, a concrete assignment which demands fulfillment.
—VIKTOR FRANKL, *MAN'S SEARCH FOR MEANING*

An existential crisis is one of the most difficult experiences to face as a physician, as it demands that the healer not only reflect personally but also prepare to accompany their patient into the raging river of complexity, seeking the unknowable answers to life's hardest questions. It calls for the readiness to engage in the ultimate creative act of a human life, death. In thinking of it, I am reminded of the quote, "there is in a life a vulnerability so extreme, a suffering so unspeakable, that it goes beyond words. In the face of such suffering, all we can do is stand in witness, so no one bear it alone."[1]

Russell was a professor of physics. Despite the burdens of a fatal and disfiguring tumor of his jaw, he remained thoroughly engaged with investigating the world around him. Russell devoted his last months and weeks of life to exploring the landscape of his inner existence. As a man of science, the unified field offered Russell a safe and sacred means to enter his mind and touch his spirit. The exploratory time was difficult, as he was asked to confront, recognize, and repair the darkest parts of himself hidden away in the recessed corners of his being.

A former alcoholic, Russell had brought harm to many, including himself, during his years of intoxication. With each part, he painfully, yet willingly, gave space for the needed healing, and each time he experienced what he described as "expansion." Russell talked of the landscape of his mind becoming richer, more open, colorful. To his great wonder and surprise, his fractured relationship with his son found new ground to rebuild.

Like the Japanese art, wabi-sabi, this imperfect relationship was reperceived and appreciated for its cracks and crevasses. From it, the beauty of a new relationship, one with his granddaughter, bloomed. Known as a very stoic and unfeeling man, Russell found himself experiencing vast emotion. He cherished each one of his tears. From raw grief to the silliest of laughter, these tears bathed him and renewed his spirit. As his body and spirit began to separate, he became more distraught. "I just don't want to miss it!" he'd exclaim with frustration.

The longing was rooted in his physicist's mind. He wanted to know and share the deep secrets of the universe. This longing was the unbearable signal for Russell to trust in the universe he had so diligently dedicated his life's work to knowing. Bearing witness to his existential crisis was one of the most challenging experiences of my career. Flooded with terror and hope, rage and wonder, awe and anguish, I would repeatedly stand with Russell at the edge of the unknown only to turn back toward the safety of his mind. Then it just happened one early winter morning: he released the identity of his scientist's mind, and with it, the longing gave way to a few hours of profound lucidity, and Russell trustfell into the universe.

The universe's trajectory points in the direction of complexity, continually evolving with breathtaking speed. If we resist the call to cocreate in support of this foundational phenomenon, we humans suffer in its wake. Longing to know *why* interferes in the flow of the present, unfolding experience, as we get trapped ruminating in the past or imagining what the future holds. The ability to escape to our minds, while a necessary component to the uniquely human capacity to create, also sets us up for the uniquely human capacity to suffer. What the Buddhists call "all-pervasive suffering," it reflects an ever-present undercurrent of longing to rectify the gap between how we perceive things to be and the true essence of reality.[2]

Longing in everyday life is often felt in the tension between living with a sense of mystery weighted with the day-to-day happenings of the material. Faced with doubt, dipping into the uncertain terrain of spiritual life requires passion and devotion. It requires all of your adult faculties. When faced with the dishes, a broken toilet, aging parents, teenage angst, or the million other things on your to-do list, it's really clear as to why contemplatives are found secluded in monasteries or caves.

The suffering of longing draws out the passionate creativity needed to devote oneself to growing toward the awareness of something much greater. Longing and arrested in development, we wait for the right time, the right space, or the right reason to embark on this last leg of our journey. Russell taught me that waiting for death to make the time, give me space, or grant the permission to devote myself in exploring my existence is ridiculous. And with his words, he entrusted me to see my devotion through: "Please make use of my suffering…be wise with your life, my dear. It's just so beautiful…"

PURPOSE: TO WHAT AM I DEVOTED?

"What's a purpose?" Freddie had asked. "A reason for being," Daniel had answered.

— LEO BUSCAGLIA, *THE FALL OF FREDDIE THE LEAF*

The Fall of Freddie the Leaf is a beautiful children's book written by author and treasured University of Southern California professor Dr. Leo Buscaglia.[3] The book exquisitely captures the language with which many are able to gracefully talk with their children about change and death. I have often gifted copies to young siblings upon the death of their brother or sister, recognizing that siblings, like their parents, have no title identifying their distinct status. Unlike orphan or widow, it seems the English language has no adequate words to express such loss and its grief.

Buscaglia was greatly affected by loss, yet he walked in a state of uninterrupted love. Following the suicide of one of his students, he facilitated a course entitled Love 1A. The noncredit course crowned him with the title "Dr. Love" and a vast international following.[4] Author of several bestselling titles, Buscaglia embodied the actualized life. In *Personhood*, Buscaglia dedicates the book in this way:

> "This book is dedicated to those who are eager to encounter themselves before their death
>
> therefore
>
> it is dedicated to *LIFE* and those *HUMAN BEINGS* who strive to give it their special meaning."[5]

Reflecting his ever-present pairing of love and loss, Buscaglia goes on to talk about the need for purpose: "Each act makes us manifest. It is what we do, rather than what we feel, or say we do, that reflects who and what we truly are. Each of our acts makes a statement as to our purpose… Anything that leads to good, to joy, to understanding, to acceptance is significant. It is this knowledge of one's ability to contribute to a universal continual and infinite productivity, that adds special meaning to our lives and courage of our mortality."[6] Often beautifully summarized, "It's not enough to have lived. We should determine to live for something…"[7]

Returning again to humanistic psychologist Scott Barry Kaufman, "Having a purpose fuels perseverance despite obstacles because perseverance is seen as worth the effort."[8] Kaufman continues, "purpose is…the overarching aspiration that energizes one's efforts and provides a central source of meaning and significance in one's life." Purpose "causes a fundamental reordering of the most central motives associated with the self... By committing to a higher aspiration, you are accepting responsibility for the consequences of your actions as you embark on the journey to fulfill your purpose."[9]

In Maslow's words, "Self-actualizing people are, without one single exception, involved in a cause outside their own skin, in something outside of themselves. They are devoted, working at something, something which is very precious to them—some calling or vocation in the old sense, the priestly sense. They are working at something which fate has called them to..."[10]

The need for purpose is seemingly asking us, *"To what are you devoted?"*

I often wonder about purpose, about the importance of a "determination to live for something," especially in the wake of my dad's suicide. I have attempted to shake off the societal and familial norms I'd learned growing up about the sin of suicide as well as my scientific understanding of taking one's life, to examine the cold, stark ethics of his decision. I have also strived to understand his choice through the lens of purpose. What was his determination, his purpose? I still have found no answers. But I do know his legacy of pain leaves the choice in my hands—of how to live with it, to make meaning of it, to transform it—to determine its purpose and how it informs the purpose of my own life.

Emily Esfahani Smith, author and psychologist, has spent her entire career studying meaning. Initially, her research interest was about finding happiness, but as she reveals in her 2017 TED Talk, "the data showed that chasing happiness can make people unhappy. And what really struck [her] was this: the suicide rate has been rising around the world, and it recently reached a thirty-year high in America. Even though life is getting objectively better by nearly every conceivable standard, more people feel hopeless, depressed, and alone. There's an emptiness gnawing away at people, and you don't have to be clinically depressed to feel it. Sooner or later, I think we all wonder: *Is this all there is?* And according to the research, what predicts this despair is not a lack of happiness. It's a lack of something else, a lack of having meaning in life."[11]

Ringing with devotion, Smith's work confirms that meaning is "belonging to and serving something beyond yourself and from developing the best within you." She sees four pillars in meaning: storytelling, belonging, purpose, transcendence. So much of what we experience in suffering is about meaning, particularly the stories we have about our lives. Nearing the end of her presentation, Smith says something simple but striking: "But living a meaningful life takes work. It's an ongoing process. As each day goes by, we're constantly creating our lives, adding to our story. And sometimes we can get off track."[12]

Contextually, I am drawn to Viktor Frankl's work, *Man's Search for Meaning*. In it, he says, "When the primary will to meaning is frustrated, our energies are projected into the will to power, and if that need is frustrated, energy is projected into the will to pleasure."[13] So parallel to the sufferings of spirit, self, and survival, it is hard not to make the connection. Frankl having survived Auschwitz, believed that "What matters...is not the meaning of life in general but rather the specific meaning of a person's life at any given moment."[14]

Similar to Smith, Frankl names the tension I think my dad had been grappling with. The story of his life, in that moment, was seemingly off track, and the consequence was fatal. Every day, his absence reminds me, even when, mostly when, things are oppressively hard, that in each act, each moment, I must devote myself to living my life with meaning and purpose.

PLAYING WITH PASSION
The road to virtue is too hard. To master them, we must be driven by passion...
— DANIEL LIEBERMAN, SPELLBOUND

Purpose, like intimacy, demands more of us. Maslow appeared to appreciate this in the motivations of the sufferings of spirit, as he states, "Self-actualization is hard work... It involves a calling to service from the external, day-to-day world, not only a yearning from within."[15] Motivated by more than the sufferings of self and survival, people who live to actualize operate from values inherent to the needs of being—Values like "truth, goodness, beauty, justice, meaningfulness, playfulness, aliveness, uniqueness, excellence, simplicity, elegance, and wholeness."[16]

Maslow speaks further: "Higher needs are more specifically human, but no less instinctual or biological than basic needs," they do "promote greater biological efficiency... more subjective satisfaction...[pervasive] love...and are pro-socially generative." However, "higher needs have less ability to dominate, organize, and press into their service the autonomic reactions and other capacities of the organism... Higher needs are less urgent, subjectively. They are less perceptible, less unmistakable, more easily confounded with other needs by suggestion, imitation, by mistaken belief or habit."[17]

Higher needs not only require devotion—aspiration and perseverance—but they also require passion.

In 2013, psychologist and MacArthur Fellow Angela Duckworth gave her now well-known TED Talk on grit. In her book of the same name, Duckworth defines purpose as "the intention to contribute to the well-being of others."[18] Reinforcing the prepotent nature of compassion to invoke the emergence of purpose, it only makes sense that the unmet need for purpose and the suffering of longing are transformed by Duckworth's grit, a one-two punch of "perseverance and passion."[19]

Duckworth summarizes the concept of passion as "a little bit of discovery, followed by a lot of development, and then a lifetime of deepening."[20] Like previously noted in our discussion of curiosity, Duckworth also insists on another "P": play. *Before hard work comes play.* Before those who've yet to fix on a passion are ready to spend hours a day diligently honing skills, they must goof around, triggering and retriggering interest." Quoting interest expert Paul Silva, Duckworth defines interest as "the desire to learn new things, to explore the world, to seek novelty, to be on the lookout for change and variety—it's a basic drive."[21]

However, interest can get easily hijacked. In everyday life, we are assailed with endless varieties of new things. In every moment of our existence, our triumvirate brain is constantly taking in an unending stream of external events and internal information to create the direct experiences of life. To this end, Duckworth invokes William James's wisdom in his *Talks to Teachers,* where his discourse on attention brings us full circle:

> "The total mental efficiency of a [person] is the resultant of the working together of all [human] faculties. [Humans are] too complex a being for any one of them to have the casting vote. If any one of them do have the casting vote, it is more likely to be the strength of his desire and passion, the strength of interest."[22]

Seemingly, playing with passion is the final tool essential to living an actualized life.

To summarize the importance of playing with passion to mitigate the suffering of longing, "If we've chosen our purpose wisely, we can intentionally shift our priorities and reorganize our strivings so that they help serve a common purpose, enabling us to transcend our current selves and move toward our best possible selves." Further quoting Kaufman, he goes on to speak of the perseverance of passion in terms of striving: "Striving wisely involves choosing overarching strivings that (a) really fit your deepest growth impulses, (b) feel enjoyable and are freely chosen, (c) help you move toward a future self that will continue to grow and contribute to society, and (d) are well integrated with your other strivings in life as well as your other basic needs."[23]

Needless to say, satisfying our need for purpose requires daily devotion to muster the energy required to pursue passion. Below is a simple daily needs inquiry to support your growth. Walking through each need, it aims to identify your present moment sufferings and where you may need to direct the day's attention:

> Sit comfortably in a place where you feel safe and undistracted for the duration of the inquiry. Have a notepad and pencil or pen near your space. Know at any time during the inquiry, you can choose to stop. Should you choose to stop, explore what prompted your decision. Perhaps free write, walk, or stretch to help slow the process down. Feel free to restart when comfortable.
>
> Begin with recognizing the present moment. Pick up your external senses, note what you smell, taste, hear. What is touching your skin. What do your eyes see? Take in each sense individually and then let them go, allowing all your senses to open and receive.
>
> Close your eyes or unfocus the gaze toward the space at the end of your nose. Turn your attention inward and pick up your internal senses. What thoughts and feelings do you notice? Any emotions? Again, take in each inner sense and then let them go, allowing thoughts, feelings, emotions to flow through you.
>
> With a deep breath, now shift your attention to the bottom of the feet and toes. Notice any feelings, sensations, thoughts, or images that arise as you

attend to the bottom of your feet. Linger as long as necessary. When ready, slowly move attention to the top of the feet and ankles.

Attend to the feet and ankles. Again noticing feelings, sensations, and thoughts that arise. No need to analyze, just notice. Linger as long as you need and, when ready, shift attention to the lower legs and knees.

Attend to the lower legs and knees. Attend, notice and, when ready, shift to the upper legs.

Attend to the upper legs. Attend, notice and, when ready, shift to hips and pelvis.

Attend to the hips, pelvis, and buttocks. Again notice and attend to any feelings, sensations, and thoughts that may arise. Take as long as necessary.

Taking a deep breath, now expand your attention to take in the whole of your lower body.

Silently inquire: **Am I *safe*?**

Notice, allow, and attend to anything that may arise: thoughts, feelings, emotions, sensations.

Is *fear* present? If so, to what extent is it influencing the feeling of *stability*?

Attend. Allow.

If you find your attention wandering, just gently return to the present.

With a deep breath, shift attention to focus on the lower abdomen and sacrum. Take the time to attend and allow for direct experience to arise.

Silently inquire: **Do I *matter*?**

Notice, allow, and attend to anything that may arise: thoughts, feelings, emotions, sensations.

Is *shame* present? If so, to what extent does it influence the feeling of *belonging*?

Attend. Allow.

Note any attachments to feelings, thoughts, sensations; gently let them go and return to the present.

Now take a moment to attend to the breath.

Focus on your needs for safety and connection; clarify. Are you hungry, anxious, angry, apathetic, lonely, tired? Recognize and relax into what is arising. Allow it to be there. Investigate sensations, feelings, emotions, moods, thoughts. Nurture and note what you need.

Take in a few deep breaths.

Release the breath and allow it to take its natural rhythm in the body.

Rest in open receptivity, gently returning to the present as necessary.

With a deep breath, shift attention to the central abdomen and mid-back. Attend and allow.

Silently inquire: **Who *am* I?**

Recognize, allow, and attend to anything that may arise: thoughts, feelings, emotions, sensations.

Is a feeling of *ignorance* or confusion present? If so, to what extent does it influence a feeling of *knowingness*?

Attend. Allow. Note Attachments.

If you find your attention wandering or attached, make use of your agency to return to the present.

When ready, with the next breath, move attention to the heart center, chest, upper back, arms, and hands. Attend and allow. Thoughts, feelings, emotions, sensations will arise, no need to analyze.

Silently inquire: **Am I willing to *grow*?**

Continue to recognize, attend, and allow. Let go of attachments. Use agency to return to the present.

Is there a feeling of *judgment*? If so, to what extent is it influencing your *curiosity*?

Honor your aspirations.

Now take a moment to attend to the breath.

Remain here, attending and allowing for esteem and exploration needs to be further clarified. Spend time with sensations, feelings, emotions, thoughts. What orientation will the day take—toward safety or toward growth? Nurture and note what you need.

Take in a few deep breaths.

Release the breath and allow it to take its natural rhythm in the body.

Rest in open receptivity, gently returning to the present as necessary.

With the breath and aspirations in hand, attention now moves to the neck, throat, jaw and mouth, ears, and nose.

Silently inquire: **Do I fully *accept* myself?**

Again, recognize, attend, and allow.

Is there a feeling of *isolation*? If so, to what extent is it influencing your feelings of *compassion*?

Notice, allow, and attend to anything that may arise: thoughts, feelings, emotions, sensations. Let go of attachments. Accept all that flows your way.

If you find your attention wandering, just gently return to the inquiry.

With the next breath, shift to attend to the eyes, forehead, and scalp.

Silently inquire: **To what am I *devoted*?**

Recognize, allow, and attend to anything that may arise: thoughts, feelings, emotions, sensations.

Is there a feeling of *longing*? If so, how is it blurring your inner *wisdom*?

Attending, allowing, letting go of attachments, accepting. Take your time.

Breathe.

Remain here to clarify your needs for intimacy and purpose. Open to the universal senses, receive with no expectation. Spend time with images, insights, intuition, sensations, feelings, emotions, thoughts. Integrated and whole, nurture and note what you need.

To close the session, take in a deep breath, then starting at the top of the head, slowly move attention down over the scalp, face, neck, and throat. Breathe and move attention over the shoulders and upper back to the arms and hands. Breathe. Attention moves to the heart and mid-back. Breathe, down to the abdomen and low back. Attention moves with breath. To hips and pelvis, upper legs. Down to knees, lower legs, and ankles. And, with one deep breath, ground your feet.

Silently repeat:

I am safe. I do matter. I know who I am. I am growing. I am accepting, and I am wise.

Return to the breath, pick it up to deepen it for a few rounds. Upon releasing the breath to its natural rhythm, expand your attention to capture the whole of your body.

Silently inquire: What will be my focus for today? How is it calling my attention?

Slowly open your eyes or refocus your gaze.

With little effort, pick up your notepad and pen/pencil and jot down what your inquiry revealed.

Safety:
Am I SAFE? ← Fear —|—|—|—→ Stability

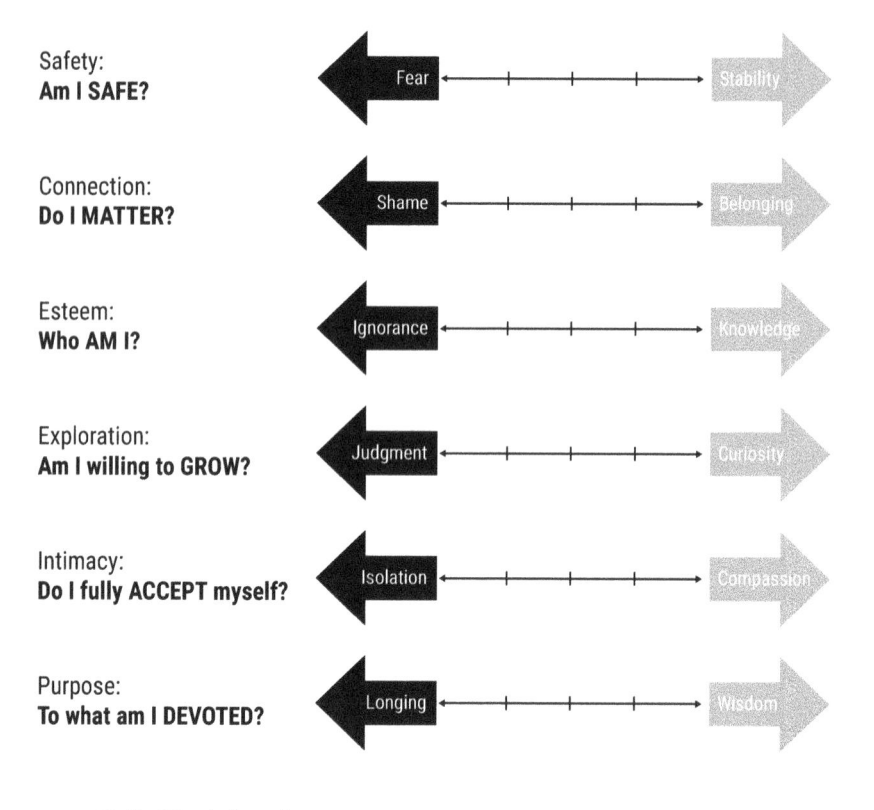

Connection:
Do I MATTER? ← Shame —|—|—|—→ Belonging

Esteem:
Who AM I? ← Ignorance —|—|—|—→ Knowledge

Exploration:
Am I willing to GROW? ← Judgment —|—|—|—→ Curiosity

Intimacy:
Do I fully ACCEPT myself? ← Isolation —|—|—|—→ Compassion

Purpose:
To what am I DEVOTED? ← Longing —|—|—|—→ Wisdom

Daily Needs Inquiry

AWARENESS

If you bring forth what is within you, what you bring forth will save you. If you don't bring forth what is within you, what you don't bring forth will destroy you.

— GOSPEL OF THOMAS

William James's notion of total mental efficiency, achieved through the integration of all of our developmental faculties, highlights the final dimension of neuroscience and its relationship to suffering—consciousness. Every tradition has words for this part of who we are—spirit, soul, essence, animating force, élan vital, I am-ness, Self with a capital S, etc. In the scientific realms, it is named consciousness. While we are still in our infancy of understanding, a good working definition of consciousness might be "simply the light by which the contours of mind and body are known...never improved or harmed by what it knows."[24]

Awareness is the unique human faculty to recognize consciousness and stabilize it as a way of being. Transcendence is living in and from it. For me, awareness is simply the "being" part of human being.

The neurobiological correlates of consciousness and the mind's awareness of it are being intensely studied. Interestingly but probably not surprisingly, some of our greatest science on consciousness is happening in the study of death and dying. Circling back to the work of Dr. Sam Parnia, he and his colleagues have discovered something earth-shattering. It seems our consciousness remains intact after death.

Just a bit of background: This research has found that our brains elicit increasing periods of high oscillating gamma waves as we approach death. Gamma waves are the strongest of the brain's electrical signatures that we can capture on electroencephalogram (EEG). Unlike the other brain waves, gamma is the only frequency found in every part of the brain, indicative of the brain's ability to synchronize and integrate information from all networks and quadrants. In everyday life, we see blips of gamma when we have the wonder of a eureka moment—that instant when you solve a problem or take in a bite of a new food.[25]

As we already discussed, when death approaches, we undergo an "internal transcendent, hyperconscious, lucid experience." This gamma wave experience not only increasingly happens throughout dying but reappears with intensity in the moments following the cessation of heart function and perceived physical death. Studies have shown this phenomenon to last for minutes and as long as a couple hours. The lucid hours prior to Russell's death were one of the longest examples of this phenomenon I have had in my own practice. Often called terminal lucidity, Parnia describes it as the "activation of…otherwise dormant brain pathways…[unlocking] access to parts of our hidden consciousness…[suggesting] human consciousness may be potentially far vaster than we can ordinarily perceive…"[26]

But it seems death is not the only place we've been able to detect high gamma. We have also seen it in meditation. Work done by neuroscientist Richard Davidson, in partnership with psychologist Daniel Goleman and His Holiness the fourteenth Dali Lama, Tenzin Gyatso, has found a "special state of consciousness…described in the classical meditation literature centuries ago, which is that there is a state of being which is not like our ordinary state. Sometimes it's called liberation, enlightenment, awake, whatever the word may be, we suspect there's really no vocabulary that captures what that might be…it's very spacious and you're wide open, you're prepared for whatever may come, we just don't know. But we do know it's quite remarkable."[27]

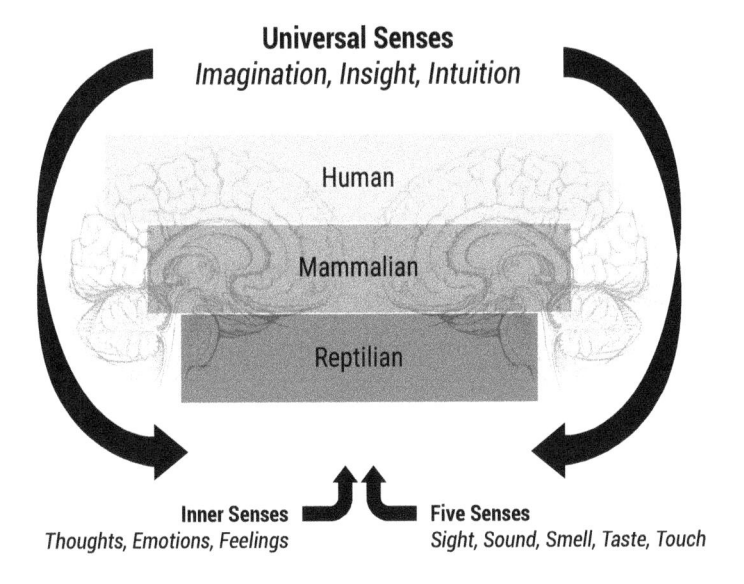

Universal Senses
Imagination, Insight, Intuition

Human

Mammalian

Reptilian

Inner Senses
Thoughts, Emotions, Feelings

Five Senses
Sight, Sound, Smell, Taste, Touch

While on the extreme, both sets of research demonstrate that we can actively exercise our minds to open to these extraordinary states. As consequence of our universal senses, we are equipped for what researchers define as transcendent experiences—"transient mental states marked by decreased self-salience and increased feelings of connectedness."[28]

While imagination—"whatever you're thinking about when whatever you're thinking about isn't actually there in front of you"—is familiar to all of us; insight and intuition are less so.[29] Both insight and intuition speak to the various ways the brain attempts to integrate the conscious and unconscious. Insights are related to those eureka moments noted above, where a conscious thought process receives information from the unconscious to give us a solution. Intuition, on the other hand, erupts without warning from the unconscious, giving us a feeling of "explicit awareness."[30]

Where the traditional five senses allow us to interact with the external world, and our inner senses of thoughts, emotions, and feelings are the doors to our internal world, the universal senses are the gateway to the vastness of the conscious world. Together these sensory experiences manifest in a "unitary continuum" of transcendent functions, "ranging from the experience of becoming deeply absorbed in an engrossing book, sports performance, or creative activity to…the great mystical illumination."[31]

To this end, my direct experiences with death and dying as well as those with deep meditation have led me to believe that creativity is the expressive power of consciousness. Creativity is the mystery's manifestation in the human world of material and complexity. Elizabeth Gilbert opens her book, *Big Magic: Creative Living Beyond Fear,* with a beckoning call and answer:

> "Q: What is creativity?
>
> A: The relationship between a human being and the mysteries of inspiration."[32]

With her signatory cheeky wisdom, Gilbert gives us the permission to engage with creativity's power. Encouraging us toward a "charmed, interesting, passionate existence."[33] Or, in more scientific terms, an existence that demonstrates an "openness to one's inner life, a preference for complexity and ambiguity, an unusually high tolerance for disorder and disarray, the ability to extract order from chaos… unconventionality, and a willingness to take risks."[34]

There is a social myth that a creative life requires suffering, with the tormented artist serving as the iconic archetype.[35] While not a causal relationship, there does seem to be correlation, especially if you take the view that suffering is the manifestation of an unmet need. Suffering may not be required for creativity, but seemingly, a willingness to engage with it is. Creativity demands the full breadth of experiences. Creativity necessitates all of our developmental tasks of prediction, pause, perspective, paradox, and perseverance. Creativity serves to reveal our purpose to which it asks us to devote our lives in passionate pursuit.

An astute saying, never confirmed but often attributed to Albert Einstein, says, "The intuitive mind is a sacred gift, and the rational mind is a faithful servant. We have created a society that honors the servant and has forgotten the gift."[36] Creative minds generate original ideas and work "to make them valuable to society."[37] When we map the system of creative characteristics to the developmental need framework of suffering and satisfaction, the parallels are unmistakable. The developmental trajectory rockets us toward creativity, which some argue is our species' universal condition and purpose on this planet.

WISDOM

We do not receive wisdom, we must discover it for ourselves, after a journey through the wilderness which no one else can make for us, which no one can spare us, for our wisdom is the point of view from which we come at last to regard the world.
— MARCEL PROUST, *IN SEARCH OF LOST TIME VOL. II*

Complexity is the evolutionary by-product of the perpetual cycle of creation, transformation, and dissolution. In humans, this cycle plays out at each level of our existence—minute to minute, experience to experience, life season to life season. Taken to its extreme, death appears to be the most creative act of a human life. Our need for purpose propels humans' ability to actively participate in all that life has to offer, including death.

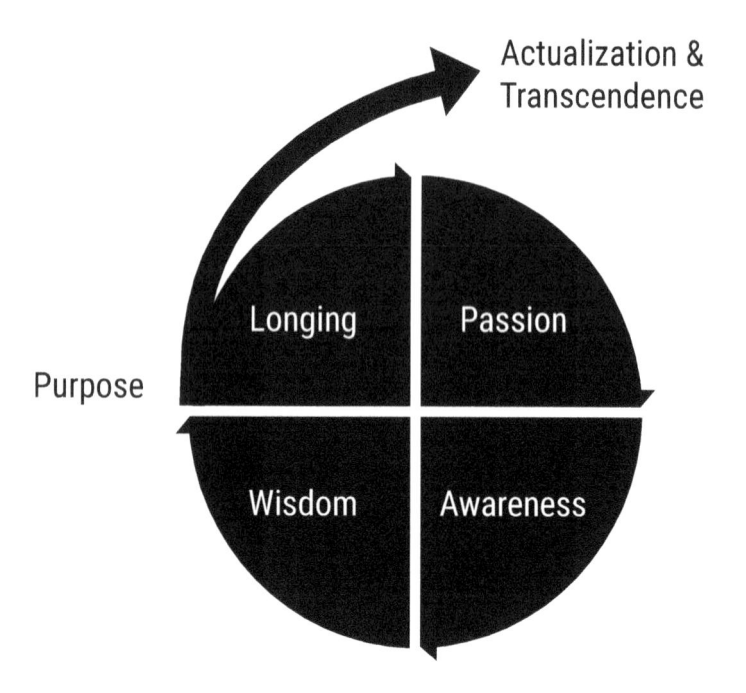

The suffering of longing points us to the need for purpose. Transformed by perseverance and passion, longing gives rise to awareness. At the highest level of human development, we function in a state of authentic interdependence, and from it, knowledge is transformed into wisdom.

Devoted, we begin the shift from interdependence to transcendence, and awareness stabilizes toward actualization. Instinct, intellect, and intuition are merged. Body and mind no longer split, all seamlessly integrated in the aware spirit.

A form of death and rebirth, we are able to transcend the follies of our human nature, step into our roles as cocreators, and flourish in the light of wisdom.

PART 3:

SUFFERING AND SELF-ACTUALIZATION

Transcendence

People have a hard time letting go of their suffering. Out of fear of the unknown, they prefer suffering that is familiar.

—THICH NHAT HANH

The memory of caring for a young man named Westly will forever be burned on my heart. Petite, doe-eyed, and bespectacled, Westly flitted about his room like a hummingbird in flight. West was living with pancreatic cancer, and it had reached the last stages. While his physical pain was manageable, his heartache of having to let go of his life was unbearable. He loved his life, wholeheartedly, and those around him loved him too. As a man who graciously carried the wounds of his childhood abuse and neglect, West served as a counselor in an organization for kids enduring homelessness. West was married, having wed his husband just a few short years prior to his diagnosis. A deeply loving blended family—some of origin, some of choice—surrounded the couple. As he approached his last days, West became very restless, pacing all hours of the night and day. His faith was calling him to take the leap it demands of all its believers, and he felt helpless in how to "just do it." He even got a new pair of white and gold Nike sneakers for inspiration.

Though sitting was rare in those moments, his husband invited West to rest just for a few minutes to talk with me about his pending leap of faith. Animated, he described his repeated vision of being at the precipice, toes just over the edge, reaching toward a cloud-filled void that beckoned him with a low hum of love and sorrow. In describing the hum, he closed his eyes and rested back in his bed. A wellspring of tears suddenly rushed forth. Flooded with gratitude, West continued to weep and laugh. Inquiring about what was holding him back from leaning into the cloud of hum, West described what appeared to be three apron strings tethering him to this life. West remained resting for a few more moments, quieted in his vision, and we held space. Glassy-eyed, curious and yearning, West awoke and wanted to make meaning of the apron strings.

We talked about how each of us must call back the parts of us unhealed from our past, incorporating the lessons they bring with their retrieval. West understood and reported that over the last handful of weeks he had revealed and welcomed the remaining secrets of his life into the present and felt whole in his existence. With suggestion, West then began to list out the most important roles and identities of his life, his husband capturing them with pen and paper. In reviewing the beautiful list, I asked if any of the roles felt incomplete. West quickly identified three. Looking up with the sorrow-filled gaze of wisdom, West knew what remained for him to do. We worked with his vision and created a weighty pair of golden scissors that would appear when he was ready to cut his apron strings.

West never left his bed again. Over the afternoon, family and friends quietly filtered through the room, each receiving a kiss and smile from their beloved West. That night, together with his husband, West drew lines through the remaining roles and identities in his life, and he drifted peacefully into the hum.

The realm of death, historically relegated to our philosophical and religious traditions, is now opening its doors to the scientific tradition. The language of the bardos and reincarnation, of purgatory, heaven, and hell, of sacredness, the collective unconscious and even God is filling the pages of scientific study as it never has before. With more and more of us engaging with the meaning in mortality, the line between life and death becomes very blurry, at times, obliterated.

Maslow's words on mortality salience: "It is quite clear that we are always suffering from this cloud that hangs over us, this fear of death. If you can transcend the fear of death, which is possible—if I could now assure you of a dignified death instead of an undignified one, of a gracious, reconciled, philosophical death...your life today, at this moment, would change. And the rest of your life would change. Every moment would change."[1]

So why wait? From this viewpoint, death is the ultimate creative experience of a human life. In reimagining its purpose, we now understand suffering's invitation to the transcendent. While alive, we are undoubtably subject to the moment-to-moment whims of chaos. Needs become urgently compromised, several may vie for our attention, and our suffering motivates us toward a fork in the road— one that leads to unknown change, the other circling back around to the familiarity of what is known. Signaling the different choices we have in our lives, the sufferings clue us in to which choice is most creative and pro-developmental.

In choosing the unknown, we embrace our suffering and are rewarded with creative capacities from which the death of our former self gives rise to one wholly (or holy, you choose!) new. Living in presence, actualized, new needs arise, old needs recall our attention, and the cycle begins again. Through the eyes of death, I came to understand transcendence in its ultimate form while suffering has shown me how to experience transcendence in the everyday.

Don't waste your suffering.

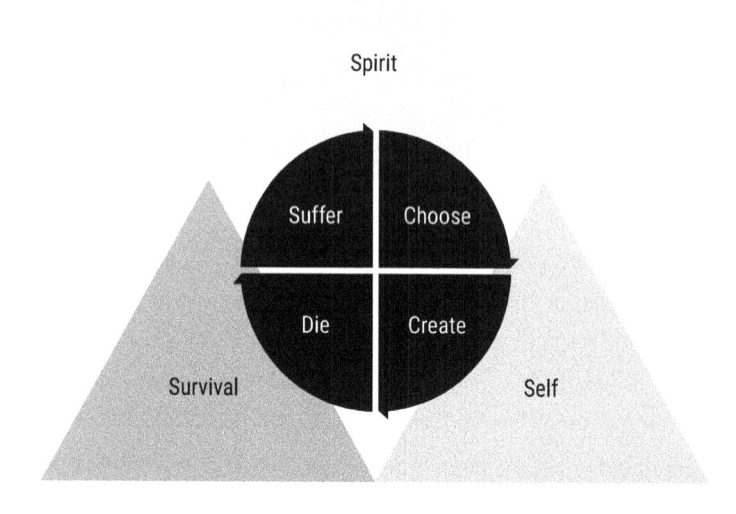

Compass of Suffering

Picking up the Compass

The Opening of Mortality reveals the map of life, as it unfolds between the events of birth and death.

The Compass of Suffering allows you to wisely navigate life through life's vacillations toward self-actualization.

The Gift of Choosing provides the opportunity for developmental qualities of actualization to emerge.

The Act of Manifesting unleashes the full potential of human creativity.

Famously, scientist Jonas Salk developed the polio vaccine. Less so, but no less meaningful, Salk was also noted for his brilliant biophilosophical perspectives on the future of our species. Picking up where Darwin left off, Salk's theory is often summarized as evolution favoring the survival of the wisest:

> "When we speak of the survival of the wisest, by wisest we mean those who comprehend the survival-evolutionary

process, as well as the being-becoming process, and who make choices such as enhance the possibility of existence rather than nonexistence, recognizing evolution as an essential and inexorable continuum of growth and development."[1]

In *Survival of the Wisest,* Salk asserts that our species is in the midst of an evolutionary inflection point, and the book is a call for us to live differently. Updated in *A New Reality,* a collaboration with his son Jonathan, Salk's ideas describe a human epoch that embraces *tikkun olam, a* Hebrew term translated as "repair of the world." Salk beautifully envisions the "inflection point [where] human social behaviors and mores, [lead] to a much more collaborative ethos and way of doing things," and with it a hope for "a new era to which humanity could aspire."[2]

Through lands of dependence, independence, interdependence, and transcendence, the sufferings of survival, self, and spirit serve as the compass and waypoints along this journey we call life. Navigating the truths of mortality, duality, change, paradox, interconnectedness, and creativity, we learn to attend and attach, act with agency and aspiration, serve with acceptance and awareness toward the true possibility of actualization.

Death is the true north of the compass of suffering, and fear is where the journey begins. Mortality salience, "the state of conscious activation of the thoughts of death," acknowledges our impermanence while encouraging us to step toward and embrace our basic needs and instinctual fear of death. The map of life becomes clear and calls us to be present and prepare, and with practice, we learn to predict the possibilities. From prediction, the ability to attend gives rise, the suffering of fear is balanced with stability, and the need for safety is satisfied.[3]

As a social species, we are inherently dependent on our families of origin during our most vulnerable years. Our need for connection emerges to foster these essential ties. In childhood, navigating the polarities that result from the world's dualistic nature requires nurturance, protection, and guidance provided by caring adults. Sadly, nearly half of us grow into adults without adequate support. The suffering of shame points us toward the reparenting we need to develop fruitful attachments in our relationships, especially in the relationship we have to ourselves. In learning to pause, we can appreciate our emotions, shifting behavior from impulsive reactivity to responsiveness. Only then can we be assured that we matter and know to whom we belong.[4]

With our basic needs adequately met, the sufferings of survival open to the sufferings of the self. Ignorance blinds us to our essential nature, and with the knowledge of how our sense of self is constructed, we gain a new perspective that opens the faculty of agency. Equipped to be of value and effect change in the world, our development shifts toward independence.

Agency empowers choice, and the exercise of choice ushers in the suffering of judgment. Judgment, the unmet need for exploration, exists as a consequence of the pervasiveness of paradox in the human condition. In holding paradox, we understand that two conflicting things can simultaneously be true, and judgment shifts to the satisfaction of curiosity. The adult marker of aspiration then catapults our development toward interdependence, and from the satisfaction of the becoming needs emerge the needs for being.

The need for intimacy harkens the suffering of isolation in what is known as the "dark night of the soul," and perseverance is the name of the game. Here we are asked to develop the adult capacity of acceptance. By fully accepting our own histories, we can then be open to the acceptance of others. In this powerful interconnectedness, compassion, the highest of human powers, is unleashed to evolutionarily guide prosocial and cooperative well-being.

Finally, our need for purpose emerges. The suffering of longing motivates us to integrate all aspects of the self, surrendering to the universal condition of creative flow. Purpose-driven action reveals the inborn wisdom in all of us known as awareness. The stability of awareness launches the transcendent function and actualization unfolds.

This is your call. Pick up the compass and suffer. Suffer well.

Actualization Series

	SUFFER	CHOOSE	CREATE	DIE
Dependence, Basic Needs, and the Sufferings of Survival				
Fear	Safety	INSTINCT	Am I SAFE?	Practicing Prediction	Attention	Stability	Mortality
Shame	Connection	IMPULSE	Do I MATTER?	Invoking the Pause	Attachment	Belonging	Duality/Contrast
Independence, Becoming Needs, and the Sufferings of Self				
Ignorance	Self-Esteem	IMPERATIVE	Who AM I?	Gaining Perspective	Agency	Knowledge	Change
Judgement	Exploration	INTENTION	Am I willing to GROW?	Holding Paradox	Aspiration	Curiosity	Paradox
Interdependence, Being Needs, and the Sufferings of Spirit				
Isolation	Intimacy	INSPIRATION	Do I fully ACCEPT myself?	Committing to Perservere	Acceptance	Compassion	Interconnectedness
Longing	Purpose	IMAGINATION, INSIGHT, INTUITION	To What Am I DEVOTED?	Playing with Passion	Awareness	Wisdom	Creativity
Transcendence			Live in Presence	Actualization		

Acknowledgments

To my husband, Christian, and my children, Elyse and Cian, thank you. Thank you for tolerating my early mornings and sleepless nights. Thank you for allowing me countless hours of writing in my PJs on the porch.

To Stacey, my sister, thank you…for everything.

To Aunt Betsy, my sisters Calley and Shannon, my mom, and extended family, thank you for all the things you've done to help get me here. God knows it wasn't easy!

To all my dear friends, especially Tracy Spears and Kelley Scott, for your time, energy, and personal investment in bringing *Suffer.* to a reality, I will forever be grateful.

To my teachers, especially Dr. Tamara Vesel and Mrs. Alice Arlen. You both appeared like angels to guide my life when I needed it most.

To patients, colleagues, and students, your lives are the inspiration in these pages. Thank you for trusting my care.

A big thank you to the entire Manuscripts team, especially Chrissy, Zen, Sarah, Cooper, Shanna and Eric. To my fellow Cohort 23 writers…we did it!

To everyone who preordered *Suffer.* and made its publishing possible, thank you, thank you!

End Notes

A NOTE BEFORE BEGINNING

1. Lidia Yuknavitch, *The Misfit's Manifesto* (New York, NY: TED Books, 2017), 101.

2. Ibid.

SUFFER. CHOOSE. CREATE. DIE.

1. Brené Brown, *Atlas of the Heart: Mapping Meaningful Connection and the Language of Human Experience* (New York, NY: Random House, 2021), 90.

THE PROBLEM OF SUFFERING

1. Andrew Juniper, *Wabi Sabi: The Japanese Art of Impermanence* (Rutland, VT: Tuttle, 2003).

2. Eric J. Cassell, "The Nature of Suffering and the Goals of Medicine," *New England Journal of Medicine* 306, no. 11 (March 1982): 639–645, DOI: 10.1056/NEJM198203183061104.

3. Rui Yi Gan, "The Second Arrow of Suffering," *Age of Awareness* (blog), December 14, 2021, https://medium.com/@kurtganruiyi/the-second-arrow-of-suffering-2640bf239694.

4. Eric J. Cassell, "The Nature of Suffering and the Goals of Medicine," *New England Journal of Medicine* 306, no. 11 (March 1982): 639–645, DOI: 10.1056/NEJM198203183061104.

5. Tyler Tate and Robert Pearlman, "What We Mean When We Talk about Suffering—and Why Eric Cassell Should Not Have the Last Word," *Perspectives in Biology and Medicine* 62, no. 1 (Winter 2019): 95–110, DOI: 10.1353/pbm.2019.0005.

6. Tyler J. VanderWeele, "Suffering and Response: Directions in Empirical Research," *Social Science & Medicine* 224 (March 2019): 58–66, DOI: 10.1016/j.socscimed.2019.01.041.

A NEW PARADIGM OF SUFFERING

1. David Foster Wallace, *This Is Water: Some Thoughts, Delivered on a Significant Occasion, about Living a Compassionate Life* (New York, NY: Little, Brown & Company, 2009), 4.

2. Liz Boehm, "Mitigate Leader Loneliness," (Webinar, Heart of Safety Insights Huddle, CEO Coalition, March 28, 2024), https://www.stryker.com/content/m/hsc/en/index/contact.html.

3. Alexander Atkins, "Best Commencement Speeches: David Foster Wallace," *Atkins Bookshelf* (blog), June 4, 2021, https://atkinsbookshelf.wordpress.com/tag/best-commencement-speeches/.

4. David Foster Wallace, *This Is Water: Some Thoughts, Delivered on a Significant Occasion, about Living a Compassionate Life* (New York, NY: Little, Brown & Company, 2009), 4.

5. Abraham H. Maslow, "A Theory of Human Motivation," *Psychological Review* 50, no. 4 (1943): 370–396, https://psychclassics.yorku.ca/Maslow/motivation.htm.

6. Stan van Hooft, "Suffering and the Goals of Medicine," *Medicine, Health Care and Philosophy* 1, no. 2 (May 1998): 125–132, DOI: 10.1023/a:1009923104175.

THE COMPASS OF SUFFERING

1. Scott Barry Kaufman, *Transcend: The New Science of Self-Actualization* (New York, NY: TarcherPerigee, 2020), xiii–xxxix.

2. Ibid., xxx.

3. Scott Barry Kaufman, *Transcend: The New Science of Self-Actualization* (New York, NY: TarcherPerigee, 2020), xxxi.

4. Abraham H. Maslow, "A Theory of Human Motivation," *Psychological Review* 50, no. 4 (1943): 370–396, https://psychclassics.yorku.ca/Maslow/motivation.htm.

5. Ibid.

6. Abraham H. Maslow, "A Theory of Human Motivation," *Psychological Review* 50, no. 4 (1943): 370–396, https://psychclassics.yorku.ca/Maslow/motivation.htm.

7. Ibid.

8. Abraham H. Maslow, "A Theory of Human Motivation," *Psychological Review* 50, no. 4 (1943): 370–396, https://psychclassics.yorku.ca/Maslow/motivation.htm.

9. Scott Barry Kaufman, *Transcend: The New Science of Self-Actualization* (New York, NY: TarcherPerigee, 2020), xxx.

10a. Elie Wiesel, *A Jew Today* (New York, NY: Random House, 1978), 105–106.

10b. Jack Kornfield, "The Ancient Heart of Forgiveness," *Greater Good Magazine*, August 2011, https://greatergood.berkeley.edu/article/item/the_ancient_heart_of_forgiveness.

BASIC NEEDS AND THE SUFFERINGS OF SURVIVAL

1. Bruce D. Perry and Oprah Winfrey, *What Happened to You?: Conversations on Trauma, Resilience, and Healing* (New York, NY: Flatiron Books, 2021), 27–30.

2. Bruce D. Perry, "The Neurosequential Model of Therapeutics: Application of a Developmentally Sensitive and Neurobiology-Informed Approach to Clinical Problem Solving in Maltreated Children," in *Infant and Early Childhood Mental Health: Core Concepts and Clinical Practice,* eds. Kristie Brandt, Bruce Perry, Stephen Seligman, and Ed Tronick (Washington, DC: American Psychiatric Publishing, Inc., 2014), 21–53.

3. Jill Bolte Taylor, *Whole Brain Living: The Anatomy of Choice and the Four Characters That Drive Our Life* (New York, NY: Hay House, 2021), 75–102.

4. Gavin de Becker, *The Gift of Fear: Survival Signals That Protect Us from Violence* (New York, NY: Back Bay Books, 2021), 324.

5. Ibid., 89.

6. Vincent J. Felitti et al., "Relationship of Childhood Abuse and Household Dysfunction to Many of the Leading Causes of Death in Adults: The Adverse Childhood Experiences (ACE) Study," *American Journal of Preventative Medicine* 14, no. 4 (May 1998): 245–258, https://doi.org/10.1016/s0749-3797(98)00017-8.

7. Teju Ravilochan, "The Blackfoot Wisdom That Inspired Maslow's Hierarchy," *Resilience* (blog), June 18, 2021, https://www.resilience.org/stories/2021-06-18/the-blackfoot-wisdom-that-inspired-maslows-hierarchy/.

8. Ibid.

9. Teju Ravilochan, "The Blackfoot Wisdom That Inspired Maslow's Hierarchy," *Resilience* (blog), June 18, 2021, https://www.resilience.org/stories/2021-06-18/the-blackfoot-wisdom-that-inspired-maslows-hierarchy/.

10. Abraham H. Maslow, "Critique of Self-Actualization Theory," *The Journal of Humanistic Education and Development* 29, no. 3 (March 1991): 103–108, DOI: 10.1002/j.2164-4683.1991.tb00010.x.

11. Ibid.

12. Scott Barry Kaufman, *Transcend: The New Science of Self-Actualization* (New York, NY: TarcherPerigee, 2020), xxiii.

13. Ruth Whippman, "Where Were We While the Pyramid Was Collapsing? At a Yoga Class," *Society* 54 (October 2017): 527–529, DOI: 10.1007/s12115-017-0203-0.

14. Bruce D. Perry and Oprah Winfrey, *What Happened to You?: Conversations on Trauma, Resilience, and Healing* (New York, NY: Flatiron Books, 2021), 279–285.

15. Ibid., 142.

FEAR.

1. Gavin de Becker, *The Gift of Fear: Survival Signals That Protect Us from Violence* (New York, NY: Back Bay Books, 2021), 1–25.

2. Abraham H. Maslow, "A Theory of Human Motivation," *Psychological Review* 50, no. 4 (1943): 370-96, https://psychclassics.yorku.ca/Maslow/motivation.htm.

3. Ernest Becker, *The Denial of Death* (New York, NY: Free Press, 2023), 87.

4. Ibid., xxviii and 27.

5. Dean Mobbs et al., "On the Nature of Fear," *Scientific American*, November 2019, https://www.scientificamerican.com/article/on-the-nature-of-fear/.

6. Jill Bolte Taylor, *Whole Brain Living: The Anatomy of Choice and the Four Characters That Drive Our Life* (New York, NY: Hay House, 2021), 81.

7. Gavin de Becker, *The Gift of Fear: Survival Signals That Protect Us from Violence* (New York, NY: Back Bay Books, 2021), 318–326.

8. Bruce D. Perry and Oprah Winfrey, *What Happened to You?: Conversations on Trauma, Resilience, and Healing* (New York, NY: Flatiron Books, 2021), 84–91.

9. Ibid.

10. Bruce D. Perry and Oprah Winfrey, *What Happened to You?: Conversations on Trauma, Resilience, and Healing* (New York, NY: Flatiron Books, 2021), 90–91.

11. Ibid.

12. Bruce D. Perry and Oprah Winfrey, *What Happened to You?: Conversations on Trauma, Resilience, and Healing* (New York, NY: Flatiron Books, 2021), 90–91.

13. Richard Wilkinson, "How Economic Inequality Harm Societies," July 2011, TEDGlobal, TED video, 00:16:37, https://www.ted.com/talks/richard_wilkinson_how_economic_inequality_harms_societies?language=en&trigger=15s&subtitle=en.

14. Adam Grant and Barry Schwartz, "Too Much of a Good Thing: The Challenge and Opportunity of the Inverted U," *Perspectives on Psychological Science* 6, no. 1 (January 2011): 61, DOI: 10.1177/1745691610393523.

15. Feeding America, "Hunger Facts," *Hunger in America* (blog), Feeding America, accessed July 4, 2024, www.feedingamerica.org/hunger-in-america.

16. Paul Bloom, *The Sweet Spot: The Pleasures of Suffering and the Search for Meaning* (New York, NY: Ecco, 2021), 82.

17. David A. Kessler, *The End of Overeating: Taking Control of the Insatiable American Appetite* (Emmaus, PA: Rodale Books, 2010), xv–xxvii.

18. Kory Taylor, Alok K. Tripathi, and Elizabeth Jones, "Adult Dehydration," in *StatPearls [Internet]* (Treasure Island, FL: StatPearls Publishing, 2024), https://www.ncbi.nlm.nih.gov/books/NBK555956/.

19. National Heart, Lung, and Blood Institute, "What Are Sleep Deprivation and Deficiency?" *Health Topics* (blog), National Institutes of Health, accessed August 13, 2024, https://www.nhlbi.nih.gov/health/sleep-deprivation.

20. Eric Suni and Alex Dimitriu, "What Is 'Revenge Bedtime Procrastination'?" *Sleep Health* (blog), Sleep Foundation, December 8, 2023, https://www.sleepfoundation.org/sleep-hygiene/revenge-bedtime-procrastination.

21. Matthew Walker, "Everything You Know about Sleep Is Wrong with Dr. Matthew Walker," *The Science of Success Podcast*, released January 4, 2018, 01:06:44, https://www.successpodcast.com/show-notes/2018/1/3/everything-you-know-about-sleep-is-wrong-with-dr-matthew-walker.

22. Jill Bolte Taylor, *Whole Brain Living: The Anatomy of Choice and the Four Characters That Drive Our Life* (New York, NY: Hay House, 2021), 78.

23. Gavin de Becker, *The Gift of Fear: Survival Signals That Protect Us from Violence* (New York, NY: Back Bay Books, 2021), 318.

24. Ibid.

25. Bruce D. Perry and Oprah Winfrey, *What Happened to You?: Conversations on Trauma, Resilience, and Healing* (New York, NY: Flatiron Books, 2021), 57.

26a. Bessel van der Kolk, *Body Keeps the Score: Brain, Mind, and Body in the Healing of Trauma* (London, UK: Penguin, 2015).

26b. Antonio Damasio, *The Feeling of What Happens* (Boston, MA: Mariner Books, 2000).

27. Bessel van der Kolk, *Body Keeps the Score: Brain, Mind, and Body in the Healing of Trauma* (London, UK: Penguin, 2015), 4.

28. Ibid.

29. Antonio Damasio, *The Feeling of What Happens* (Boston, MA: Mariner Books, 2000), 262.

30. Gavin de Becker, *The Gift of Fear: Survival Signals That Protect Us from Violence* (New York, NY: Back Bay Books, 2021), 19.

31. Ibid., 331.

32. Gavin de Becker, *The Gift of Fear: Survival Signals That Protect Us from Violence* (New York, NY: Back Bay Books, 2021), 117 and 331.

33. Ibid., 329 and 320.

34. Gavin de Becker, *The Gift of Fear: Survival Signals That Protect Us from Violence* (New York, NY: Back Bay Books, 2021), 331.

35. Bruce D. Perry and Oprah Winfrey, *What Happened to You?: Conversations on Trauma, Resilience, and Healing* (New York, NY: Flatiron Books, 2021), 146–147.

36. American Heart Association, "Advanced Cardiovascular Life Support (ACLS)," *Courses and Kits* (blog), American Heart Association, accessed July 4, 2024, https://cpr.heart.org/en/cpr-courses-and-kits/healthcare-professional/acls.

37. Gavin de Becker, *The Gift of Fear: Survival Signals That Protect Us from Violence* (New York, NY: Back Bay Books, 2021), 57.

38. Amishi Jha, *Peak Mind: Find Your Focus, Own Your Attention, Invest 12 Minutes a Day* (New York, NY: HarperOne, 2021), 6, HarperCollins Kindle Edition.

39. *The Stanford Encyclopedia of Philosophy*, Winter 2021 (Stanford, CA: Stanford University, 2021), s.v. "Attention," https://plato.stanford.edu/archives/win2021/entries/attention/.

40. William James, *The Principles of Psychology* (New York, NY: Henry Holt and Company, 1890).

41. Dan Siegel, "12 Revolutionary Strategies to Nurture Your Child's Developing Mind, Survive Everyday Parenting Struggles, and Help Your Family Thrive," *Dr. Dan Siegel's Blog* (blog), accessed July 4, 2024, https://drdansiegel.com/whole-brain-child-handouts/.

42. Jack Kornfield, *The Wise Heart: A Guide to the Universal Teachings of Buddhist Psychology* (New York, NY: Bantam Books, 2009), 227.

43. Abraham H. Maslow, "A Theory of Human Motivation," *Psychological Review* 50, no. 4 (1943): 370–396, https://psychclassics.yorku.ca/Maslow/motivation.htm.

SHAME.

1. Bruce D. Perry and Oprah Winfrey, *What Happened to You?: Conversations on Trauma, Resilience, and Healing* (New York, NY: Flatiron Books, 2021), 50.

2. Steven J. Cooper, "From Claude Bernard to Walter Cannon. Emergence of the Concept of Homeostasis," *Appetite* 51, no. 3 (November 2008): 419–427, DOI: 10.1016/j.appet.2008.06.005.

3a. Bruce D. Perry and Oprah Winfrey, *What Happened to You?: Conversations on Trauma, Resilience, and Healing* (New York, NY: Flatiron Books, 2021), 62–65.

3b. David A. Kessler, *The End of Overeating: Taking Control of the Insatiable American Appetite* (Emmaus, PA: Rodale Books, 2010), xv–xxvii.

4. Bruce D. Perry and Oprah Winfrey, *What Happened to You?: Conversations on Trauma, Resilience, and Healing* (New York, NY: Flatiron Books, 2021), 50.

5. Scott Barry Kaufman, *Transcend: The New Science of Self-Actualization* (New York, NY: TarcherPerigee, 2020), 43.

6. Amrisha Vaish, Tobias Grossmann, and Amanda Woodward, "Not All Emotions Are Created Equal: The Negativity Bias in Social-Emotional Development," *Psychological Bulletin* 134, no. 3 (May 2008): 383–403, DOI: 10.1037/0033-2909.134.3.383.

7. Brené Brown, *Atlas of the Heart: Mapping Meaningful Connection and the Language of Human Experience* (New York, NY: Random House, 2021), 134–142.

8. Ibid.

9. Gavin de Becker, *The Gift of Fear: Survival Signals That Protect Us from Violence* (New York, NY: Back Bay Books, 2021), 324.

10. Nigel Benson, Catherine Collin, Joannah Ginsburg, Voula Grand, Merrin Lazyan, and Marcus Weeks, *The Psychology Book: Big Ideas Simply Explained* (New York City, NY: DK Publishing, 2024), 236, Kindle.

11. Scott Barry Kaufman, *Transcend: The New Science of Self-Actualization* (New York, NY: TarcherPerigee, 2020), xix.

12. Brené Brown, *The Gifts of Imperfection: Let Go of Who You Think You're Supposed to Be and Embrace Who You Are* (Center City, MN: Hazelden Publishing, 2010), xiii.

13. Brené Brown, *Atlas of the Heart: Mapping Meaningful Connection and the Language of Human Experience* (New York, NY: Random House, 2021), 134–142.

14. Steven F. Maier and Martin E. Seligman, "Learned Helplessness: Theory and Evidence," *Journal of Experimental Psychology: General* 105, no. 1 (July 1976): 3–46, DOI: 10.1037/0096-3445.105.1.3.

15. US Surgeon General, *Our Epidemic of Loneliness and Isolation: The U.S. Surgeon General's Advisory on the Healing Effects of Social Connection and Community* (Washington, DC: Office of the US Surgeon General, 2023), https://www.hhs.gov/sites/default/files/surgeon-general-social-connection-advisory.pdf.

16. Brené Brown, "Dr. Vivek Murthy on Loneliness and Connection," *Unlocking Us Podcast,* released April 21, 2020, 00:56:19, https://brenebrown.com/podcast/dr-vivek-murthy-and-brene-on-loneliness-and-connection/#transcript.

17. Julianne Holt-Lunstad, Theodore F. Robles, and David A. Sbarra, "Advancing Social Connection as a Public Health Priority in the United States," *American Psychologist* 72, no. 6 (September 2017): 517–530, DOI: 10.1037/amp0000103.

18. John Cacioppo, "The Lethality of Loneliness: John Cacioppo at TEDxDesMoines," TEDx Talks, September 9, 2013, 00:18:44, https://www.youtube.com/watch?v=_ohxlo3JoAo.

19. Stephanie Cacioppo et al., "Loneliness and Implicit Attention to Social Threat: A High-Performance Electrical Neuroimaging

Study," *Cognitive Neuroscience* 7, no. 1–4 (January–October 2016): 138–159, DOI: 10.1080/17588928.2015.1070136.

20. Daniel J. Siegel, *Mind: A Journey to the Heart of Being Human* (New York, NY: W. W. Norton and Company, 2016), 188.

21. Brené Brown, *Atlas of the Heart: Mapping Meaningful Connection and the Language of Human Experience* (New York, NY: Random House, 2021), 134–142.

22. Gordon L. Flett, "An Introduction, Review, and Conceptual Analysis of Mattering as an Essential Construct and an Essential Way of Life," *Journal of Psychoeducational Assessment* 40, no. 1 (February 2022): 3–36, DOI: 10.1177/07342829211057640.

23. Jack Kornfield, *The Wise Heart: A Guide to the Universal Teachings of Buddhist Psychology* (New York, NY: Bantam Books, 2009), 227.

24. Gavin de Becker, *The Gift of Fear: Survival Signals That Protect Us from Violence* (New York, NY: Back Bay Books, 2021), 106–192.

25. Ibid., 117–268.

26. Jonathan Haidt, *The Anxious Generation: How the Great Rewiring of Childhood Is Causing an Epidemic of Mental Illness* (New York, NY: Penguin Press, 2024), 21–45.

27. Brené Brown, *The Gifts of Imperfection: Let Go of Who You Think You're Supposed to Be and Embrace Who You Are* (Center City, MN: Hazelden Publishing, 2010), 36.

28. Jill Bolte Taylor, *Whole Brain Living: The Anatomy of Choice and the Four Characters That Drive Our Life* (Carlsbad, CA: Hay House, 2021).

29. Judson Brewer, *The Craving Mind: From Cigarettes to Smartphones to Love—Why We Get Hooked & How We Can Break Bad Habits* (New Haven, CT: Yale University Press, 2018), 31.

30. Paul P. Ekman, "Basic Emotions," in *Handbook of Cognition and Emotion*, eds. T. Dalgleish and MJ Power (New York, NY: John Wiley & Sons Ltd., 1999), 45–60.

31. Paul Ekman, "Mood vs. Emotion: Differences & Traits," *Paul Ekman Group's Blog* (blog), accessed July 9, 2024, https://www.paulekman.com/blog/mood-vs-emotion-difference-between-mood-emotion/.

32. Naravana Manjunatha, Christoday Raja Jayant Khess, and Dushad Ram, "The Conceptualization of Terms: 'Mood' and 'Affect' in Academic Trainees of Mental Health," *Indian Journal of Psychiatry* 51, no. 4 (October–December 2009): 285–288, DOI: 10.4103/0019-5545.58295.

33. *APA Dictionary of Psychology,* (Washington, DC: American Psychological Association, 2008), s.v. "feeling," https://dictionary.apa.org/feeling.

34. Paul P. Ekman, "Basic Emotions," in *Handbook of Cognition and Emotion*, eds. T. Dalgleish and MJ Power (New York, NY: John Wiley & Sons Ltd., 1999), 45–60.

35a. Brené Brown, *Atlas of the Heart: Mapping Meaningful Connection and the Language of Human Experience* (New York, NY: Random House, 2021), 134–142.

35b. John A. Terrizzi, "On the Origin of Shame: Feelings of Disgust toward the Self," (PhD dissertation, West Virginia University, 2013), 134, https://researchrepository.wvu.edu/etd/134.

36. Jill Bolte Taylor, *Whole Brain Living: The Anatomy of Choice and the Four Characters That Drive Our Life* (Carlsbad, CA: Hay House, 2021), 270.

37. Bruce D. Perry and Oprah Winfrey, *What Happened to You?: Conversations on Trauma, Resilience, and Healing* (New York, NY: Flatiron Books, 2021), 48–50.

38. Robin Wall Kimmerer, *Braiding Sweetgrass: Indigenous Wisdom, Scientific Knowledge, and the Teaching of Plants* (Minneapolis, MN: Milkweed Editions, 2013), 4–10.

39. John Cacioppo, "The Lethality of Loneliness: John Cacioppo at TEDxDesMoines," TEDx Talks, September 9, 2013, 00:18:44, https://www.youtube.com/watch?v=_ohxlo3JoAo.

40. Ibid.

41. The Attachment Project Staff, "Bowlby and Attachment Theory: Insights and Legacy," *The Attachment Project's Blog* (blog), accessed August 27, 2024, https://www.attachmentproject.com/attachment-theory/john-bowlby/.

42. Scott Barry Kaufman, *Transcend: The New Science of Self-Actualization* (New York, NY: TarcherPerigee, 2020), 17–18.

43. Dorothy Heard, Brian Lake, and Una McCluskey, *Attachment Therapy with Adolescents and Adults: Theory and Practice Post Bowlby* (Oxford, England: Taylor & Francis Group, 2012), 50.

44. Gavin de Becker, *The Gift of Fear: Survival Signals That Protect Us from Violence* (New York, NY: Back Bay Books, 2021), 260–262.

45. Dorothy Heard et al., *Attachment Therapy with Adolescents and Adults: Theory and Practice Post Bowlby* (Oxford, England: Taylor & Francis Group, 2012), 78.

46. Scott Barry Kaufman, *Transcend: The New Science of Self-Actualization* (New York, NY: TarcherPerigee, 2020), 22–23.

47. Brené Brown, "Dr. Vivek Murthy on Loneliness and Connection," *Unlocking Us Podcast,* released April 21, 2020, 00:56:19, https://brenebrown.com/podcast/dr-vivek-murthy-and-brene-on-loneliness-and-connection/#transcript.

48. Linda Graham, *Bouncing Back: Rewiring Your Brain for Maximum Resilience and Well-Being* (Novato, CA: New World Library, 2013), 134.

49. Brené Brown, *Atlas of the Heart: Mapping Meaningful Connection and the Language of Human Experience* (New York, NY: Random House, 2021), 134–142.

50. Ibid.

51. Norman Cousins, *The Anatomy of an Illness: As Perceived by the Patient* (New York, NY: W.W. Norton & Company, 2005), 148.

52. Brené Brown, *Atlas of the Heart: Mapping Meaningful Connection and the Language of Human Experience* (New York, NY: Random House, 2021), 134–142.

53. Alice B. Huang and Howard Berenbaum, "Accepting Our Weaknesses and Enjoying Better Relationships: An Initial Examination of Self-Security," *Personality and Individual Differences* 106, no. 1 (February 2017): 64–70, DOI: 10.1016/j.paid.2016.10.031.

54. Daniel J. Siegel, *Mind: A Journey to the Heart of Being Human* (New York, NY: W. W. Norton and Company, 2016), 188.

55. Scott Barry Kaufman, *Transcend: The New Science of Self-Actualization* (New York, NY: TarcherPerigee, 2020), 118–121.

BECOMING NEEDS AND THE SUFFERINGS OF SELF

1. René Descartes, *A Discourse on the Method*, trans. Ian MacLean (Oxford, England: Oxford University Press, 2008).

2. Edward G. Miner Library Staff, "Robert Adler, PhD.," Faculty Collections, University of Rochester Medical Center, accessed July 24, 2024, https://www.urmc.rochester.edu/libraries/miner/rare-books-and-manuscripts/archives-and-manuscripts/faculty-collections/the-papers-of-robert-ader-ph-d.aspx.

3. Lynn Hunt, "The Self and Its History," *The American Historical Review* 119, no. 5 (December 2014): 1576–1586, DOI: 10.1093/ahr/119.5.1576.

4. Daniel Z. Lieberman, MD, *Spellbound: Modern Science, Ancient Magic, and the Hidden Potential of the Unconscious Mind* (Dallas, TX: BenBella Books, 2022), 14.

5. Roberto Assagioli, *Subpersonalties: A Collection of Articles,* eds. Kenneth Sørensen, Jan Kuniholm, trans. Gordon Symons (Denmark: Kentaur Publishing, 2022), 7–8.

6. Richard C. Schwartz, *No Bad Parts: Healing Trauma & Restoring Wholeness with the Internal Family Systems Model* (Boulder, CO: Sounds True, 2021), 2.

7. Ibid., 8.

8. David Foster Wallace, *This Is Water: Some Thoughts, Delivered on a Significant Occasion, about Living a Compassionate Life* (New York, NY: Little, Brown & Company, 2009), 53.

9. Richard C. Schwartz, *No Bad Parts: Healing Trauma & Restoring Wholeness with the Internal Family Systems Model* (Boulder, CO: Sounds True, 2021), 13.

10. Abraham H. Maslow, *Motivation and Personality* (New York, NY: Harper & Row, 1954), 129.

11. Daniel Z. Lieberman, MD, *Spellbound: Modern Science, Ancient Magic, and the Hidden Potential of the Unconscious Mind* (Dallas, TX: BenBella Books, 2022), 66.

12. Scott Barry Kaufman, *Transcend: The New Science of Self-Actualization* (New York, NY: TarcherPerigee, 2020), xxx.

IGNORANCE.
1. Abraham H. Maslow, *The Farther Reaches of Human Nature* (New York, NY: Viking Press, 1971), 28.

2. Scott Barry Kaufman, *Transcend: The New Science of Self-Actualization* (New York, NY: TarcherPerigee, 2020), 59.

3. Ibid.

4. David Foster Wallace, *This Is Water: Some Thoughts, Delivered on a Significant Occasion, about Living a Compassionate Life* (New York, NY: Little, Brown & Company, 2009), 4.

5. Jack Kornfield, *The Wise Heart: A Guide to the Universal Teachings of Buddhist Psychology (*New York, NY: Bantam Books, 2009), 225-226.

6. Daniel Z. Lieberman, MD, *Spellbound: Modern Science, Ancient Magic, and the Hidden Potential of the Unconscious Mind* (Dallas, TX: BenBella Books, 2022), 54.

7. Daniel Kahneman, *Thinking, Fast and Slow* (New York, NY: Farrar, Straus, and Giroux, 2011), 20-24.

8. Ibid.

9. Daniel Z. Lieberman, MD, *Spellbound: Modern Science, Ancient Magic, and the Hidden Potential of the Unconscious Mind* (Dallas, TX: BenBella Books, 2022), 68-73.

10. Richard C. Schwartz and Robert R. Falconer, *Many Minds, One Self: Evidence for a Radical Shift in Paradigm* (Oak Park, IL: Trailheads—Center for Self Leadership, 2017), 153–158.

11. Ibid., 17.

12. Richard C. Schwartz, *No Bad Parts: Healing Trauma & Restoring Wholeness with the Internal Family Systems Model* (Boulder, CO: Sounds True, 2021), 73–82.

13. Francis Weller, *The Wild Edge of Sorrow: Rituals of Renewal and the Sacred Work of Grief* (New York, NY: North Atlantic Books, 2015), xix.

14. Ed Diener, Richard E. Lucas, and Christie N. Scollon, "Beyond the Hedonic Treadmill: Revising the Adaptation Theory of Well-Being," *American Psychologist* 61, no. 4 (May–June 2006): 305–314, DOI: 10.1037/0003-066X.61.4.305.

15. J. Krishnamurti, *The Book of Life: Daily Meditations with J. Krishnamurti* (San Francisco, CA: HarperOne, 1995), "April 9."

16. Ibid., "February 14."

17. Gavin de Becker, *The Gift of Fear: Survival Signals That Protect Us from Violence* (New York, NY: Back Bay Books, 2021), 251.

18. Scott Barry Kaufman, *Transcend: The New Science of Self-Actualization* (New York, NY: TarcherPerigee, 2020), 60–61.

19. Ibid.

20. Roberto Assagioli, *Subpersonalties: A Collection of Articles,* eds. Kenneth Sørensen, Jan Kuniholm, trans. Gordon Symons (Denmark: Kentaur Publishing, 2022), 7–8, https://kennethsorensen.dk/en/product/subpersonalities-a-collection-of-articles.

21. Scott Barry Kaufman, *Transcend: The New Science of Self-Actualization* (New York, NY: TarcherPerigee, 2020), 59.

22. Ibid., 57–58.

23. Dallas Cullen and Lisa Gotell, "From Orgasms to Organizations: Maslow, Women's Sexuality and the Gendered Foundations of the Needs Hierarchy," *Gender, Work, and Organizations* 9, no. 5 (November 2002): 537–555, DOI: 10.1111/1468-0432.00174.

24. Daniel Z. Lieberman, MD, *Spellbound: Modern Science, Ancient Magic, and the Hidden Potential of the Unconscious Mind* (Dallas, TX: BenBella Books, 2022), 62.

25. Scott Barry Kaufman, *Transcend: The New Science of Self-Actualization* (New York, NY: TarcherPerigee, 2020), 32.

26. Ibid., 34.

27. Brené Brown, *The Gifts of Imperfection: Let Go of Who You Think You're Supposed to Be and Embrace Who You Are* (Center City, MN: Hazelden Publishing, 2010), xi.

JUDGMENT.

1. Oprah Winfrey, "The Powerful Lesson Maya Angelou Taught Oprah," October 19, 2011, Oprah Winfrey Network, Oprah's LifeClass, video, 00:04:16, https://www.oprah.com/oprahs-lifeclass/the-powerful-lesson-maya-angelou-taught-oprah-video.

2. Daniel Z. Lieberman, MD, *Spellbound: Modern Science, Ancient Magic, and the Hidden Potential of the Unconscious Mind* (Dallas, TX: BenBella Books, 2022), 202.

3. Brené Brown, "Daniel H. Pink on the Power of Regret," *Dare to Lead Podcast*, released February 14, 2022, 01:13:40, https://brenebrown.com/podcast/the-power-of-regret/.

4. Jill Bolte Taylor, *Whole Brain Living: The Anatomy of Choice and the Four Characters That Drive Our Life* (New York, NY: Hay House, 2021), 23–24.

5. Ibid., 26–27.

6. Jill Bolte Taylor, *Whole Brain Living: The Anatomy of Choice and the Four Characters That Drive Our Life* (New York, NY: Hay House, 2021), 75–148.

7. Daniel Z. Lieberman, MD, *Spellbound: Modern Science, Ancient Magic, and the Hidden Potential of the Unconscious Mind* (Dallas, TX: BenBella Books, 2022), 123.

8. Scott Barry Kaufman, "Is It Time for a Personal Growth Mindset," *Scientific American Blog* (blog), November 30, 2015, https://blogs.scientificamerican.com/beautiful-minds/is-it-time-for-a-personal-growth-mindset/.

9. Delia O'Hara, "The Intrinsic Motivation of Richard Ryan and Edward Deci," *American Psychological Association's Blog* (blog), accessed August 22, 2024, https://www.apa.org/members/content/intrinsic-motivation.

10a. Anja Van den Broeck et al., "Capturing Autonomy, Competence, and Relatedness at Work: Construction and Initial Validation of the Work-Related Basic Need Satisfaction Scale," *Journal of Occupational and Organizational Psychology* 83, no. 4 (December 2010): 981–1002, DOI: 10.1348/096317909X481382.

10b. Richard M. Ryan and Edward L. Deci, "Self-Regulation and the Problem of Human Autonomy: Does Psychology Need Choice, Self-Determination, and Will?" *Journal of Personality* 74, no. 6 (December 2006): 1557–1586, DOI: 10.1111/j.1467-6494.2006.00420.x.

11. Ibid.

12. Ernest Becker, *The Denial of Death* (New York, NY: Free Press, 2023), 26.

13. Daniel Z. Lieberman, MD, *Spellbound: Modern Science, Ancient Magic, and the Hidden Potential of the Unconscious Mind* (Dallas, TX: BenBella Books, 2022), 68–71.

14. Immanuel Kant, *Kant's Critique of Judgment,* trans. by J. H. Bernard (New York, NY: Macmillan and Co., 2015), Kindle Locations 2721–2724, Project Gutenberg eBook.

15a. Paul Bloom, *The Sweet Spot: The Pleasures of Suffering and the Search for Meaning* (New York, NY: Ecco, 2021).

15b. Alyssa Monks, "How Loss Helped One Artist Find Beauty in Imperfection," November 2015, TEDxIndiana University, TED video, 00:12:59, https://www.ted.com/talks/alyssa_monks_how_loss_helped_one_artist_find_beauty_in_imperfection/transcript?subtitle=en.

16. Sir Ken Robinson, "Do Schools Kill Creativity?" February 2006, TED2006, TED Talk, 00:19:12, https://www.ted.com/talks/sir_ken_robinson_do_schools_kill_creativity/transcript?language=en.

17. *Good Will Hunting,* directed by Gus Van Sant, (1997; Miramax), 02:06:00, Apple TV Streaming.

18. Jack Kornfield, *The Wise Heart: A Guide to the Universal Teachings of Buddhist Psychology* (New York, NY: Bantam Books, 2009), 258–259.

19. Tony Bossis, "Luminous: The Terror and the Ecstasy of Psychedelics," *To the Best of Our Knowledge*, released April 8, 2023, 00:14:08, https://www.ttbook.org/show/luminous-what-can-psychedelics-teach-us-about-dying.

20. Chimamanda Ngozi Adichie, "The Danger of a Single Story," July 2009, TEDGlobal, TED Video, 00:18:32, https://www.ted.

com/talks/chimamanda_ngozi_adichie_the_danger_of_a_single_story?subtitle=en.

21. Lucas Seastrom, "Mythic Discovery Within the Inner Reaches of Outer Space: Joseph Campbell Meets George Lucas—Part 1," *Films* (blog), *Star Wars,* October 22, 2015, https://www.starwars.com/news/mythic-discovery-within-the-inner-reaches-of-outer-space-joseph-campbell-meets-george-lucas-part-i.

22. Abraham H. Maslow, *Motivation and Personality* (New York, NY: Harper & Row, 1954), 97–104.

23. Diane Ackerman, *Deep Play* (New York, NY: Vintage Books, 1999), 26.

24. Elizabeth Gilbert, *Big Magic: Creative Living Beyond Fear* (New York, NY: Riverhead Books, 2015), 238.

25. Jungian Center for the Spiritual Sciences Staff, "Jung on the Transcendent Function," *Essays* (blog), Jungian Center for the Spiritual Sciences, accessed August 11, 2024, https://jungiancenter.org/jung-on-the-transcendent-function/.

BEING NEEDS AND THE SUFFERINGS OF SPIRIT

1. Scott Barry Kaufman, *Transcend: The New Science of Self-Actualization* (New York, NY: TarcherPerigee, 2020), xxvi.

2. Scott Barry Kaufman, "Self-Actualizing People in the Twenty-First Century: Integration with Contemporary Research on Personality and Well-Being," *Journal of Humanistic Psychology* 63, no. 1 (January 2023): 1–33, DOI: 10.1177/0022167818809187.

3. Ibid.

4. Scott Barry Kaufman, "Self-Actualizing People in the Twenty-First Century: Integration with Contemporary Research on Personality and Well-Being," *Journal of Humanistic Psychology* 63, no. 1 (January 2023): 1–33, DOI: 10.1177/0022167818809187.

5. Brené Brown, "Defining Spirituality," *Brené Brown* (blog), March 27, 2018, https://brenebrown.com/articles/2018/03/27/defining-spirituality/.

6. Jack Kornfield, *The Wise Heart: A Guide to the Universal Teachings of Buddhist Psychology* (New York, NY: Bantam Books, 2009), 7–8.

ISOLATION.

1. Angeles Arrien, *The Second Half of Life* (Boulder, CO: Sounds True, 2005), 81.

2. Dr. Ryan Messatzzia, "Erik Erikson on Intimacy vs Isolation (Psychosocial Stages of Development)," Dr. Ryan Messatzzia, March 16, 2024, 00:01:57, https://www.youtube.com/watch?v=a2tkXPDURGU.

3. Erik Erikson, "Notes on the Life Cycle," *Ekistics* 32, no. 191 (October 1971): 260–265, https://www.jstor.org/stable/43619203.

4. Carl G. Jung, *Man and His Symbols,* ed. M.L. von Franz (New York, NY: Anchor Press, 1964), 167.

5. Alan Watts, "Tribute to Carl Jung," 1960, Pacifica Radio, Marin County, CA, audio recording, 00:28:30, Waking Up App.

6. Raven Montmorency, "'The Dark Night of the Soul': A Poem by St. John of the Cross on Using Afflictions for Greater Spiritual Growth," *Nspirement* (blog), March 14, 2020, https://nspirement.com/2020/03/14/the-dark-night-of-the-soul-a-poem-by-st-john-of-the-cross-on-using-afflictions-for-greater-spiritual-growth2.html.

7. Todd B. Kashdan, David J. Disabato, Fallon R. Goodman, and Patrick E. McKnight, "The Five-Dimensional Curiosity Scale Revised (5DCR): Briefer Subscales while Separating General Overt and Covert Social Curiosity," *Personality and Individual Differences* 157, no. 15 (April 2020): 1–10, DOI: 10.1016/j.paid.2020.109836.

8. Elizabeth Gilbert, *Big Magic: Creative Living Beyond Fear* (New York, NY: Riverhead Books, 2015), 13–21.

9. Angeles Arrien, *The Second Half of Life* (Boulder, CO: Sounds True, 2005), 73.

10. Jennifer McNulty, "From Asexuality to Heteroflexibility: Twenty-First Century Ushers in a New Openness About Intimate Relationships," *Newscenter* (blog), UC Santa Cruz, November 15, 2018, https://news.ucsc.edu/2018/11/hammack-relationships.html.

11. Vivek Murthy, MD, *Together: The Healing Power of Human Connection in a Sometimes Lonely World* (New York, NY: HarperCollins, 2020), 40.

12. Scott Barry Kaufman, *Transcend: The New Science of Self-Actualization* (New York, NY: TarcherPerigee, 2020), 118–120.

13. Ibid.

14. Viktor E. Frankl, *Man's Search for Meaning* (Boston, MA: Beacon Press, 2006), 104.

15. Lucas Seastrom, "Mythic Discovery Within the Inner Reaches of Outer Space: Joseph Campbell Meets George Lucas—Part 1," *Films* (blog), *Star Wars,* October 22, 2015, https://www.starwars.com/news/mythic-discovery-within-the-inner-reaches-of-outer-space-joseph-campbell-meets-george-lucas-part-i.

16. Raymond A. Moody Jr., *Life after Life: The Investigation of a Phenomenon—Survival of Bodily Death* (New York, NY: HarperOne, 2015).

17. Sam Parnia et al., "Guidelines and Standards for the Study of Death and Recalled Experiences of Death—A Multidisciplinary Consensus Statement and Proposed Future Directions," *Annals of The New York Academy of Sciences* 1511, no. 1 (May 2022): 5–21, DOI: 10.1111/nyas.14740.

18. Sam Parnia, MD, PhD, *Lucid Dying: The New Science Revolutionizing How We Understand Life and Death* (New York, NY: Hachette Books, 2024), 83.

19. Ibid., 60–62.

20. Anderson Cooper, "Stephen Colbert: Grateful for Grief," *All There Is with Anderson Cooper,* released September 21, 2022,

00:54:00, https://www.cnn.com/audio/podcasts/all-there-is-with-anderson-cooper/episodes/ae2f9ebb-1bc6-4d47-b0f0-af17008dcd0c.

21. James Hillman, *The Soul's Code: In Search of Character and Calling* (New York, NY: Ballantine Books, 1996), 10.

22. Rachel Stern, "Freudenfreude: Why We Should All Embrace This Made-Up German Word," *Learn about Germany* (blog), *The Local de,* December 2, 2022, https://www.thelocal.de/20221202/freudenfreude-why-we-should-all-embrace-this-made-up-german-word.

23. Scott Barry Kaufman, *Transcend: The New Science of Self-Actualization* (New York, NY: TarcherPerigee, 2020), 118–120.

24. Kristin Neff, "Kristin Neff: Three Components of Self-Compassion," Greater Good Science Center, October 16, 2014, 00:06:18, https://www.youtube.com/watch?v=11U0h0DPu7k.

25. John Cacioppo, "The Lethality of Loneliness: John Cacioppo at TEDxDesMoines," TEDx Talks, September 9, 2013, 00:18:44, https://www.youtube.com/watch?v=_0hxlo3JoA0.

26. Robert J. Sternberg, "Love," *Robert J. Sternberg's Blog* (blog), accessed August 17, 2024, https://www.robertjsternberg.com/love.

27. Yuval Noah Harari, "What Explains the Rise of Humans?" June 2015, TEDGlobal, London, TED Talk, 00:16:58, https://www.ted.com/talks/yuval_noah_harari_what_explains_the_rise_of_humans?subtitle=en.

LONGING.

1. Jack Kornfield, *The Wise Heart: A Guide to the Universal Teachings of Buddhist Psychology* (New York, NY: Bantam Books, 2009), 246.

2. Lion's Roar Staff, "What Are the Three Types of Suffering?" *Lion's Roar's Blog* (blog), May 20, 2024, https://www.lionsroar.com/buddhism-by-the-numbers-the-three-kinds-of-suffering/.

3. Leo Buscaglia, *The Fall of Freddie the Leaf: A Story of Life for All Ages* (Thordare, NJ: SLACK Incorporated, 1982).

4. Steven Short, "About Dr. Buscaglia," Leo Buscaglia, accessed August 19, 2024, https://www.buscaglia.com/about-dr-buscaglia/.

5. Leo Buscaglia, *Personhood: The Art of Being Fully Human* (Thordare, NJ: SLACK Incorporated, 1978), Dedication.

6. Leo Buscaglia, *Personhood: The Art of Being Fully Human* (Thordare, NJ: SLACK Incorporated, 1978), "Foreword."

7. Steven Short, "About Dr. Buscaglia," Leo Buscaglia, accessed August 19, 2024, https://www.buscaglia.com/about-dr-buscaglia/.

8. Scott Barry Kaufman, *Transcend: The New Science of Self-Actualization* (New York, NY: TarcherPerigee, 2020), "Purpose," Kindle.

9. Ibid.

10. Abraham H. Maslow, *The Farther Reaches of Human Nature* (New York, NY: Viking Press, 1971), 43.

11. Emily Esfahani Smith, "There's More to Life than Being Happy," April 2017, TED2017, TED Talk, 00:12:08, https://www.ted.com/talks/emily_esfahani_smith_there_s_more_to_life_than_being_happy?subtitle=en.

12. Ibid.

13. Viktor E. Frankl, *Man's Search for Meaning: An Introduction to Logotherapy* (Boston, MA: Beacon Press, 1962), 107.

14. Ibid., 108.

15. Scott Barry Kaufman, *Transcend: The New Science of Self-Actualization* (New York, NY: TarcherPerigee, 2020), "Purpose," Kindle.

16. Ibid., "Peak Experiences."

17. Abraham H. Maslow, *Motivation and Personality* (New York, NY: Harper & Row, 1954), 129.

18. Angela Duckworth *Grit: The Power of Passion and Perseverance* (New York, NY: Scribner, 2016), "Purpose," Kindle.

19. Ibid.

20. Angela Duckworth *Grit: The Power of Passion and Perseverance* (New York, NY: Scribner, 2016), "Interest," Kindle.

21. Ibid.

22. William James, *Talks to Teachers on Psychology: And to Students on Some of Life's Ideals* (New York, NY: Henry Holt and Company, 1925), "Attention," Project Gutenberg eBook.

23. Scott Barry Kaufman, *Transcend: The New Science of Self-Actualization* (New York, NY: TarcherPerigee, 2020), "Purpose," Kindle.

24. Sam Harris, *Waking Up: A Guide to Spirituality without Religion* (New York, NY: Simon & Schuster, 2014), 206.

25. Emiliano Santarnechhi et al. "Gamma tACS over the Temporal Lobe Increases the Occurance of *Eurkea! Moments,*" *Nature, Scientific Reports* 9, no. 5778 (April 2019): 1–12, DOI: 10.1038/s41598-019-42192-z.

26. Sam Parnia, MD, PhD, *Lucid Dying: The New Science Revolutionizing How We Understand Life and Death* (New York, NY: Hachette Books, 2024), 92.

27. Daniel Goleman, "Superhuman Brain Waves," accessed August 29, 2024, Institute for Organizational Science and Mindfulness, educational video, 00:03:31, https://www.iomindfulness.org/video-directory-r/superhuman-brain-waves.

28. Scott Barry Kaufman, *Transcend: The New Science of Self-Actualization* (New York, NY: TarcherPerigee, 2020), "Peak Experiences," Kindle.

29. Mike Llewellyn, "Can Imagination Be Measured?" *Ideas.TED.com* (blog), August 12, 2014, https://ideas.ted.com/can-a-test-measure-your-imagination/.

30. Richard Brock, "Intuition and Insight: Two Concepts That Illuminate the Tacit in Science Education," *Studies in Science Education* 51, no. 2 (June 2015): 127–167. DOI: 10.1080/03057267.2015.1049843.

31. Scott Barry Kaufman, *Transcend: The New Science of Self-Actualization* (New York, NY: TarcherPerigee, 2020), "Peak Experiences," Kindle.

32. Elizabeth Gilbert, *Big Magic: Creative Living Beyond Fear* (New York, NY: Riverhead Books, 2015).

33. Elizabeth Gilbert, *Big Magic: Creative Living Beyond Fear* (New York, NY: Riverhead Books, 2015), 42.

34. Scott Barry Kaufman and Carolyn Gregoire, *Wired to Create: Unraveling the Mysteries of the Creative Mind* (New York, NY: TarcherPerigee, 2015), xxiii.

35. Elizabeth Gilbert, *Big Magic: Creative Living Beyond Fear* (New York, NY: Riverhead Books, 2015), 39.

36. Ian Chadwick, "It Wasn't Einstein Who Said It…," *Scripturient* (blog), Ian Chadwick, February 25, 2012, https://ianchadwick.com/blog/it-wasnt-einstein-who-said-it/.

37. Scott Barry Kaufman and Carolyn Gregoire, *Wired to Create: Unraveling the Mysteries of the Creative Mind* (New York, NY: TarcherPerigee, 2015), xxv.

TRANSCENDENCE

1. Scott Barry Kaufman, *Transcend: The New Science of Self-Actualization* (New York, NY: TarcherPerigee, 2020), xvi.

PICKING UP THE COMPASS

1. Jonas Salk, *The Survival of the Wisest* (New York, NY: Harper & Row, 1973), 53.

2. Elizabeth H. Blackburn, PhD, "Foreword," in *A New Reality: Human Evolution for a Sustainable Future* by Jonas Salk and Jonathan Salk (Stanford, CT: City Point Press, 2018), 17–18.

3. Hyun Gong Moon, "Mindfulness of Death as a Tool for Mortality Salience Induction with Reference to Terror Management Theory," *Religions* 10, no. 6 (May 2019): 353, DOI: 10.3390/rel10060353.

4. Bruce D. Perry and Oprah Winfrey, *What Happened to You?: Conversations on Trauma, Resilience, and Healing* (New York, NY: Flatiron Books, 2021).

www.ingramcontent.com/pod-product-compliance
Ingram Content Group UK Ltd.
Pitfield, Milton Keynes, MK11 3LW, UK
UKHW031947151224
452382UK00015B/398/J